.01%

A Book of Faith, Music and Cancer

May God Bless and Keepyou. Me Colores

Letty Rocha-Peck

ISBN 978-1-64191-961-6 (paperback)
ISBN 978-1-64191-962-3 (digital)

Christian Faith Publishing, Inc.
832 Park Avenue
Meadville, PA 16335
www.christianfaithpublishing.com

Cover photo by: Jennifer Lyn

Printed in the United States of America

Contents

Acknowledgments

IT'S FUNNY HOW THINGS WORK out. There I am sitting on a rooftop terrace bar, overlooking the beach, enjoying my Cali Cream, while Jen sips her IPA and we begin to develop her company. Our conversation wanders off to my dyslexia, and how that did not stop me or my life. She stated that in her many years of working with teens, it seems that many forms of learning discrepancies have become a crutch for youth to just up and quit—"I can't read because I'm dyslexic", "I can't finish this task because I am attention deficit." What could have stopped me but didn't were variables; my faith, my environment, my friends and family, and my perseverance and determination. I believe these were the leading factors in my success.

Which leads me to thanking the people that made this possible. I want to start with Jen Bedison, because it was she that helped me realize I had a voice on paper and that it was funny. Prior to graduating from college, I always thought I was the dumbest thing on two feet. School had always been a struggle for me. But, I wanted to be a teacher. My high school counselors even told me not to go to college that, "I just wasn't made for it." But as Jen edited my twelve essays for Teacher of the Year I began to find a new gift developing. She never became tired or became impatient even on the tenth version. She never made me feel that dyslexia was a factor in my intelligence.

Becoming Teacher of the Year for San Diego taught me so many valuable lessons, but it solidified one major factor in my head, I was not dumb, I had a voice on paper and it was a gift I would use later on in my life. That is what Jen helped nurture.

Who really started it were my parents. How can you really thank them for all the self-sacrifice they did? My mom and dad did just that. Everything was for us. They were the ones who taught me, my brother and my sister our work ethics, our perseverance, our love of nature and beauty in it, our respect in others and self, and mostly our joy and happiness for life and the love for Christ. That's a pretty wonderful set of parents. They were a team, and as my friends would say, "I wanna be like Juan and Bea." They were the Ozzie and Harriet of the block, the caring Ward and June Cleaver for our friends, the funny Fred and Wilma of the clan. They made our home the welcoming Kool-Aid house for all to come.

Down the path, I continue to my sister Deb. I always wanted to do everything Debbie did. She is the funny and the brainy one. Every time Deb succeeded she was showing me the road and how to do it. It was that work ethic Juan and Bea instilled in us. Deb is the hardest working and funniest person I know. Because of her knowledge in speech and the anatomy, she helped us to understand what had happened to my voice and body. It was her role in being the scribe that deciphered and helped us grasp what the doctors were bombarding us with. She later explained to me how my vocal cords worked and what went wrong. I know God put His vocal angel as my sister.

I want to thank Adrianne Shaw for being the final voice in making me realize that "this is a good story and you should write this down." So many friends and family had already told me this, but it was Adrianne, my new magnet therapist, and later a dear friend who helped me believe that this book could be.

Along comes Nancy Alvarado to my assistance. She brought her expertise as a fellow teacher at Willow Elementary School, being a true writer, having already published several articles, working on her own book and now working for a local newspaper, to the mix. I gave Nancy a few chapters of my story to see if they would play out and if maybe it might be interesting enough to develop into a book. It was Nancy who said, "I want to feel you in the hospital! I want to be see you when you pick up your guitar for the first time after several months. Don't just tell me, make me be there with you!" Wow, she did that. Every time I was writing, I would hear her.

And then there was Kathy Applegate-Norman my twelve-hour twin from another mother. We are not two peas in a pod. She is a fair, freckled Irish type, where as I am dark brown and lean toward the Mexican–American type. Yet we hit it right off from the start of her teaching career. During our years working together we had collaborated and succeeded on several work projects. Kathy had just retired and she was the perfect full time editor I needed. I realized my limitations as a dyslexic story teller and that Kathy could help complete my thoughts on paper, as she had on our projects. I wanted her to take a more active role in my book by the cover reflecting, "written by Letty Rocha-Peck with Kathy Applegate-Norman," or "and Kathy Applegate-Norman." But she would have nothing of that. I see my book as getting written because of her. She helped decipher my thoughts and feelings when I lacked the ability. We became a team. For three years we sat on my couch in the living room and laughed and cried as she corrected my many mistakes. I never would have a book if wasn't for Kathy!

And now for my Gary, my rock, my friend, my love, my husband. I believe in the variables lining up to create an outcome. Everything had to line up, all of my life experiences, living a block away from each other as children, going to the same elementary school, going to San Diego State at the same time, living in Columbia and having cancer. He was the man, "who would want me." God has a plan for us all and Gary is part of that plan. He has enhanced my life to the fullest. We are both traveling together in our spiritual journey, which is another wonderful blessing in our life. I count Gary as another one of the many miracles in my life.

And my final thank you is the most important; it is to God. I thank Him for leading me down this journey. He has always been there in every way. Whenever I speak to someone with cancer it is the Holy Spirit that fills my mouth with the correct words. I know this was a Spirit driven project because I still do not see myself as a writer, yet each time I would sit at the computer to write the words would come pouring out. As the time passed and more words appeared on the paper, I would sit and marvel thanking God for my thoughts on the paper. I believe the Holy Spirt has led and guided me through this entire process. I know that this story will be read by the people who need to feel the hope and faith that it provides. It's how God is working in us through these modern times. We need to be open to His miracles in all the ways they are presented.

Forever I will sing, the goodness of the Lord.
—Psalm 89

Prologue

Levitation

Silly Putty? It looks like a flesh-colored balloon stretched beyond
capacity. How did they pull the skin so tight without ripping
it? Wait, where am I? Is that me on the table? How? How can
I be looking down and still be covered up flat on a bed?
I see movement,
a flurry of copper, red, black and brown!

Wow, look at all the mess, blood, and gauze. There's so
much blood and so many busy, busy people like little
ants. Dr. Schafer is busy scraping, snipping, and giving
orders. He's so calm and in deep conversation with the
other doctors. Other doctors? What other doctors?
What is that plopping sound? What did he
just put in that shiny metal bowl?
Dark, bloody chunks. Gross, was that me?
It doesn't hurt. Fascinating. Oh, look at that? Piles of coffee-colored
spores that look like mushrooms! Did that come from me?

I can't grow mushrooms inside of me!
Look at my collarbone, there's no flesh on it. It's my bare
bone. How can my body take it? Is that why I am dying?
Dying?
I'm dying?
I am not afraid.

Soothing, serene, smooth, I am at peace!
I feel the warmth of hands all over me, my arms, my
legs, and my forehead. I hear murmuring.
If I focus, I will know what they are saying.
I don't want to focus. Do I want to know? No, I want to stay here,
floating
It feels so comforting.
It is unconditional love!

Wait!

I know that smell, burning, sizzling, and clotting flesh.
Plop! Another piece of me in a dish. If I smell it, can I taste it?

It's real. Oh, the sensations! So many feelings, so powerful!

The angels are carrying me.
Am I dying?
This isn't too bad. It actually feels so wonderful.
Soft, tranquil, no cares and nothing to worry about.
I am nestled, wrapped like a baby.
Cradled.

Pine scent? Antiseptic?
Metal on metal.
Clink, clank, clip!

I don't want to go. Take me home.
Wait, what?
It's time to go? I have to go back? I'm not finished? I must wake?

God?
There really is a light?
It's so brilliant.
So glowing, warm, and soothing,
Your love is soft, like a baby kitten purring and nuzzling me.
I feel so cherished
and sheltered.
Are you sure? Okay, I understand.
I still have a lot to do.

Mercy, I am forgiven.
It's time?
I need to wake?
You know, I really don't want to go.
Can I stay?
I won't cause a ruckus.
Of course.
Sure, anything you want me to do.
I love You…and You love me.
I'm going to be okay.
It's ok. I understand You are with me, just in a different way.

My nose is getting colder.
Wow, there are a lot of people here!
Who are they? Oh, it's my mom, dad, my sister, and Joe.
They are all praying with Father Kulleck, a gruff
and curmudgeonly but caring priest.
There's the crucifix, the holy water, and his Bible.
He kisses the stole and puts it on. He's giving me the last rites.
Pain, so much pain!
I sense love and worry.
It's okay, everyone
Don't worry
I'm going to be okay!

Part 1

The Beginning

1

We're Not in Kansas Anymore

DEATH, THE ACTION OR FACT of dying or being killed, the end of the life or organism.

Really? That's where I want to start, at death? Was it over thirty-five years ago that I was looking at death's door? Was it fiction or make-believe all in my head? No, I have the scars to prove it. It was real. But what did I lose and what did I gain by that experience?

The seal is cracked open. Whoosh! The fresh air is immediately sucked out of the cabin and replaced with moist, thick, and suffocating air. I feel my body jolt with the shock of the heat and heaviness of it. It is so dense. I actually feel I can hold it in my hand.

The airline stewardess guides us to the door. She smiles and puffs air from her lips, which blew her bangs up as if to say, "Whew, we made it!" Then she thanks us for flying Air Columbia and smiles again. Her face says it all. You could almost hear her thinking, *Thank you God for not being hijacked.* I mean, it was the late seventies, and anything that flew was being skyjacked and ransomed for big bucks!

I look down the rusted iron staircase only to see two soldiers, fully loaded with giant semiautomatic or automatic or—I don't know—just really, really big rifles, pistols, and a full belt of ammunition. They are sporting uniforms, hats, and Castro-type beards and are flanking the stairs. *Oh my God! We got hijacked and now we landed in Cuba! Why is everyone so calm? Somebody do something! We are being kidnapped!*

We are escorted to the airport by a friendly man who tells us to take off our jewelry and wait right there. *This is it, we are being robbed! Don't hurt us!* He told us not to move. Someone would go rescue our luggage. *Did he say rescue?* Yes, it seems that the good guys would run after the luggage cart trying to beat out the bad guys from taking our bags. It really was a sight, sort of like a comedy where you see a ton of men running after a cart full of luggage. Bags are flying everywhere; some even flew open. Pulling, yanking, tugging, and yelling. *Oh, for sure I am in Cuba!* We watch in horror.

"My watch! My watch is gone!" one lady yells. She's with our party so I figure she's another teacher.

The man who is paid to stand by and protect us tells us that if that's all we lose, then our arrival was successful. Seems that grabbing bags at the airport is a full-time job for some. If we each got any of our luggage, then we were very lucky. *Wait, I brought a steamer trunk. Does that mean I won't be lucky?* I think, *We're not Kansas anymore, Toto. Oh man!*

Welcome to Columbia, everyone!

~Barranquilla~

It's 1978. I finally finished college. I am a teacher. I'm twenty-five and ready to set out on my own path. I had only applied at one location when a teaching job in Columbia, South America, opened up. I snatched it up and was ready for my first year of teaching in Barranquilla. In less than two weeks, I had my passport and a steamer trunk. I was set to go live in South America.

This was the first of many firsts. I lost track of counting how many firsts. Just to name a few, first time leaving home, first classroom, and first time traveling by myself. Okay, most kids might do the "home away from home" thing while in college. I didn't go away to college. I had been in the work force since the age of fifteen, and because of that, money management wasn't tricky. However, because it was Barranquilla, all foreign residents had to make sure they "saved up" a thousand dollars for the automatic exit deduction fee. I guess they figured if you were a bad citizen and tore up the place, they would get a thousand bucks from you. Since most of the foreign teachers were in bed by nine or still correcting papers, it was definitely a money-making deal for the local government.

School was good. I was amazed at my first class. We had all been instructed to never ask anyone their occupation. Most of the students had a chauffeur drop them right in front of the school then the maids would carry their books right up to the gate! They would just fly to Florida for the weekend to go to Disney World or shopping. Where did they get all this money? I don't know. We weren't allowed to ask. Being in a foreign country with very rich kids was all new to me. But our lives in Barranquilla were also a life of privilege. We went out every weekend or traveled to the little local town of Santa Marta. At Christmas, we traveled as far as Quito, Ecuador. Life was more than ample. We had everything we needed, and it was plentiful. Each teacher had an apartment, money, and friends. There was a ton of time for travel and socializing. We had what we needed and never had to squeak by.

I was thinking of staying one more year even though I missed everyone like crazy and the culture shock had not completely gone away. The school was going to give us a huge bonus for staying an additional year. Even with taxes and the money the government kept, I had a lot of money. I made over three thousand dollars my first year. I know, not much, but everything was super inexpensive there. A whole pizza was a dollar fifty, imported beer was a whopping fifty-five cents, and the local beer was thirty-five cents a can. Filet mignon was the same price as ground beef, really cheap! If I had not been so naive, I might have bought a Chanel suit for only fifty-five dollars. Best of all, I could either buy a large bottle of Tanqueray gin or an Ann Taylor dress for the same price at five dollars! The black market was alive and thriving in Barranquilla. What else did we need? I don't remember paying rent. Our money was more than ample. I came home with money to spare! If we didn't go anywhere for the weekend, we spent our time sippin' drinks poolside at the Del Prado Hotel. It was resort-style teaching all the way. That is, if you didn't account for all the weekly drug-related murders, kidnappings, and daily assaults or the fact that women were still considered second- or maybe even third-class citizens. What was really hard to get over was that a waitress had more prestige than a teacher. The food wasn't that great either. The local delicacy was a fried egg on top of a thin, beef jerky-style meat over a bed of white rice. Everyone loved it…well, almost everyone did. But we were young and carefree. We had money; we traveled; and we shopped, ate, partied, and, yes, taught. It was good living.

My folks came to visit in January because the weather was great. Upon seeing the Castro clones at the airport, my mom was so scared that she nearly kidnapped me and took me home before their vacation even got started! We enjoyed the sights of Bogota and Cartagena and had some of the best starlight meals ever. In B.Q. (Barranquilla), no one was murdered or kidnapped for the entire week they were there so I thought their stay was great; not my mom. She cried all the way back to San Diego. She couldn't believe she was leaving me there.

Sometime around February, I started to feel odd. That is really the best way to describe it. I was hot, cold, and had goose bumps. I felt sad, happy, hungry, and then not hungry. My fingernails were breaking and my skin was either dry or had permanent goose bumps, which looked exactly like a naked chicken! I had an increased heart rate and nervousness, lots of anxiety and irritability. Plus, I was always tired. My sleeping patterns were all messed up, and I kept forgetting stuff. I felt like I had permanent jet lag, sort of a brain fog. I started to eat less but I was still gaining weight. I was exercising, taking vitamins, and trying to get rest. Nothing was working. I was getting fat and cranky!

Even my bowels were whacked out. It would be okay, then for two or maybe even three days I was completely constipated enough that it even hurt. Then I would have what I called rabbit pellets or I would have more frequent bowel movements, sometimes with diarrhea. I started drinking green juices to see if that would help. I was watching everything I ate. I was obsessed with all of the oddities going on.

I also had this mind thing happening. Somewhere along the line, I decided that no one liked me anymore. I started to stay away from my friends. I wouldn't go out with them. There really wasn't much to do in Barranquilla except go out with your friends. At that time, women were still second-class citizens. A woman could not go out to a restaurant or bar without a large group of friends or with a man. If you did go out with only two or three women, then you were considered loose or maybe even a prostitute. If you didn't go out with the gang, you were left out. That was fine by me because remember, I thought they didn't like me anymore. I was stood up more than once. They tried to explain that it was a mistake, that I went one place and they another, but what they said wouldn't sink in. I really thought they did it on purpose. Wow, I was paranoid too!

Normally, I am not like that. I tend to find the good in everyone. You know, give them the benefit of the doubt, and yet, I was thinking all kinds of weird stuff about my friends. Like, they were talking about me or whispering and laughing. Crazy stuff! I wasn't being a very good friend to them either. I am sure I was very unpleasant. Lack of hormones can do that to a person. I can only think of my behavior as someone who was permanently on their menstrual cycle. Since my hormones were all messed up, I can only guess that's how I was. The thyroid influences almost every metabolic process in your body, and that's a lot!

Did I mention that I was constantly sweating? This I would chalk up to being in Barranquilla. It's really hot and humid there! If I put a bowl of potato chips out for more than ten minutes, they would be soggy and limp. We also saved on washing towels because we hardly used them. As soon as you dry yourself off from the shower, you would be soaking in perspiration.

On my first day of teaching, I thought something was running down my back. It was long and squiggly. I thought a salamander or maybe even a small snake was on my back. I really had to control myself from screaming. I carefully reached back and placed my hand on the area where I thought the creature was. They had also instructed us during our culture shock orientation to never swat at anything we may feel under our clothing. If it was an insect and we didn't kill it with the swat, then the angry bug would bite us. They told us of a man who felt something on his thigh, gently cupped his hand over whatever it was, and grabbed it slowly while pulling off his pants. Lucky for him that he did that because it turned out to be a baby scorpion. That impressed us very much. There were several kinds of poisonous insects in our area, and our instructions had been to always gently touch the area. I did. There was nothing there! It was wet. *Was that blood? Had I somehow been wounded?* No, not blood. Sweat! The sweat, was dripping down my back! Laugh if you will, but we didn't have heat like that in San Diego! Okay, so my hot flashes were easy to go unnoticed. As it turned out, that too was a symptom.

~Philosophy of Life 101 by Letty Peck~

Living in South America was what I called the character-building episode in my life. None of us have a crystal ball. I had no idea what I was preparing for while living in South America. I was doing just that, preparing for my future. I think many times, we are asked to look back at a situation and question whether we would change anything or even avoid it altogether. I would not change a thing. I would still go to teach in Barranquilla. I would not be the same person, and my reaction to any event would have been different. Barranquilla is the only place I could have honed the survival skills I would need to face my future. It was the only way I could have learned those specific lessons. It's kind of like the Prime Directive on Star Trek, which has to do with not interfering with the natural development of events. If I had not gone to Barranquilla, I still would have had cancer. Thankfully, while away, I solidified a can-do attitude. "If I did that there, then I can do this here."

~Back to My Symptoms~

I just wasn't myself. I am usually a fun, happy person but at times, I would sit on the floor between the twin beds in our studio apartment and cry in the dark. I don't even know how long I would sit there. I felt so alone and left out. Whenever I would hear the key in the lock, I would go and run to the bathroom, turn on the shower, and wipe away any signs of tears or depression. I felt ashamed for crying. She may have known but my roommate and I never talked about it. I will never know.

I was a mess. I just felt an influx of many weird feelings and emotions. I must have been hard to deal with because of the raging war that was going on in my body. Then again, maybe I wasn't too bad because at the end of the school year, we all went traveling a bit before we went back to the states. Most of us went to Panama. After that, I went to Alabama to meet my roommate's parents and then Arkansas to visit a high school friend. Through it all, the symptoms kept happening. I was good one day and then for two days, I was in a funk. I had no idea what was happening to me.

While in Columbia, I did notice a large lump forming on the left side of my neck. I really didn't know what it was because I was too much of a wreck to worry about it. I was going home in April for my brother's wedding, and I would check it out then. This lump was in the same location as a gland that would swell every time I got sick so I wasn't worried. There was another problem. As I got worse, I got fatter! I had gone from a size eight to a size twelve! It seems that everything I ate went straight to my hips. I was hardly eating but still gaining weight. Now for a twenty-five-year old, this is a big deal. All the other symptoms had gotten out of hand. I was miserable.

2

I Got the Music in Me

I HAVE STRUGGLED WITH THIS. How can I tell you this story without giving insight to my transformation? How did I go from the girl who wanted to be "cool" to a music minister, one with dedication, responsibility, and passion for Christian music? How did my goals go from a girl playing her rock guitar to someone trying to help people find the Holy Spirit through music? Most of all, how did playing this music give me the strength and drive to persevere?

~Misa Bossa Nova, Beat, Oh Yeah~

Back in 1968, I was in the seventh grade, and a brand-new happening was taking place in the Catholic church. Vatican II had finally trickled down to our little San Diego. It was the new wave for the church, a way to bring in the young people, and it was working. The altar was going to be moved so we could see it. The priest was going to face us. The mass was going to be in English or the mother language of that country. The best part for me was this thing called folk mass! Yes, it was the kumbaya era—bell-bottom pants, man on the moon, Woodstock, and "The Brady Bunch." We sang "Sugar, Sugar" by the Archie's, looked at our "Sixteen" magazines, and dreamed about Kurt Russell and Davy Jones. The Beatles gave their last rooftop concert, and I was right at the cusp of it all.

The teens at the Catholic high school right across the street from our elementary parochial school were already playing music with guitars at mass! Very modern indeed. Being in the seventh grade, we all wanted to be just like the big kids so out came the guitars. If the teens did it, then the preteens were in hot pursuit. We just knew we were going to be the next rock stars! It was the coolest thing to do.

I am not sure how the teens got their music for mass, but one of our friends had an older brother who was one of the high school rock stars. He had all the music we needed. My friend just "sorta borrowed" it and then would hand write all the words and guitar chords. When she would come to school with a new song, it was like gold. We couldn't wait to sing it. We sang "Sloop John B" by the Beach Boys and "If I Had a Hammer" by Peter, Paul and Mary. We later figured out that "Sloop John B" was not appropriate for church. We worked really hard to get enough music to fill the four music slots for mass. My friend's older brother taught us the parts of the mass. That's where the Misa Bossa Nova came into play. It was the beat, the groove, the sound, or the very special guitar strum we needed to master! It was really hard! We begged Sister to let us sing for the seventh-grade mass. "Pleeeaase, we know everything!" She kept saying to keep on practicing and that when we got good enough, we could sing at mass. My girlfriend also tormented her brother to sing with us. Then, when we got better, Sister would see that we were serious about our new musical vocation. Plus, if she saw this high school kid playing with us, then for sure we were serious and cool!

The year before, I was in the sixth grade and in public school. I remember being the lunchtime entertainment with three other friends. We sang The Monkees' songs to our peers. I guess I always wanted to be a rock star. This was better. Now I could be a rock star but in church! I still have some of that handwritten sheet music with just words and guitar chords.

We did everything the big kids did: "Day Is Done" by Peter, Paul and Mary, "Sons of God" by Ray Rep, and "Abba Father" by Carey Landry, all superstars in our new music thang. Playing guitar music during mass didn't even have a name yet. Well, maybe folk music, but the musical mass parts did and were called Misa Bossa Nova. Groovy! Later, it would be called music ministry, but then we were just being cool. It was the only reason I started to play. I wanted to be famous like the big kids, and I was!

We didn't have to sing from the choir loft any more but we got to stand up front near the altar where everyone could see us! We were special. We had rights that the other kids didn't have. We got to go to the back of the church where the priest and altar boys changed their clothes, a super big deal! We not only got out of class early, we even got to miss class altogether so we could practice! It was the big time. We were leaders of our seven-grade class. Top dogs. Far out!

Who would have known that wanting to be cool was going to be a driving force, an anchor in my survival? Music would help define me as a person. Years later, music would become so ingrained, tangled up, and embedded in me that it would seem as if they had really cut off my arm in surgery. I just can't fathom what my life would be without it.

Wait, wait! Stop the presses! Spoiler alert!

3

Who Was That Masked Man?

"Hi-ho, Silver! Away!"

When I walked into his office, I was hit by his nature. Really, I've heard people being struck down by good looks, sex appeal, a ripped bod, or a commanding presence, but nature? Was he woodsy, beachy, suave, and debonair in a desert sort of fashion? No, not really. He kind of looked like Lance Henriksen who played Abraham Lincoln in "The Day Lincoln Was Shot" or maybe you might know him better as Bishop, the android artificial life-form in "Alien" (1986). I recently saw a picture of Lance with white hair, wrinkles, and the most wonderful smile. Yes, that's pretty much how I remember him. Only then, he didn't have wrinkles or white hair, just that warm, bashful smile.

The difference between a surgeon and the Lone Ranger is that the surgeon's eyes are uncovered. You can see them clearly. The Lone Ranger covers most of his eyes with a mask, leaving just the orbs.

What does a patient really know about their surgeon? Well, only what the surgeon will unmask and share with the patient. Most of the time, we know their name and specialty. Other than that, we have little information about their personal life, especially back in the seventies when many doctors didn't even have a picture of their family in their office. There was always a distance, a mystique about the man.

There was and may still be a steadfast rule, "Don't get involved with the patient." That way, the doctor can do the job without getting attached. Thank goodness things have loosened up a bit and we are a tiny bit more familiar with the doctor. Not much, but at least now we can see pictures and maybe some artwork done by their budding kiddos. What I knew about Dr. Jeffrey Schafer? Nothing! Why take time to talk about this man who saved my life? I could have it all wrong. Maybe he's not a nice guy, just a brilliant surgeon. Maybe he's been married seventeen times because he hasn't figured out the rules to marriage. I don't really believe that. What I do remember are his eyes. He had the smoothest eyebrows and the most beautiful brown eyes with a hint of green. I don't think they qualified for hazel but very close.

This was the impression he left on me. Here is a man who had to be trained for over nine years in a specific field just to qualify to do this task. Surgeons are skilled in cutting the human body, usually for removal of unwanted things, tears, or breaks in the body. They have practiced repeatedly and learned it until it is unfailing and instinctive. We, as the patient, put our trust in them. Our lives may literally be in their hands.

Recently, I met Dr. Levy, a world-renowned surgeon who prays with his patients. This was such a new and innovative thing that he even wrote a book about his experience. Did other doctors do that before him? I don't think so. Otherwise, Dr. Levy's book would not have been a top seller. Did Dr. Schafer put my life into God's hands before he started? Maybe during the eleventh hour? I will never know. What I do know is that he was very kind and gentle with me. His whole person gave off a confidence and assurance that all would be well. His eyes shone brightly with care and compassion. He was a true and dedicated servant. While I was in the ICU, he would come in to see me several times a day. He never talked much, just checked the vitals and left. Later as I healed, I would see him once a day.

When I was sent to another doctor after I was better, I missed him. I was also a little scared because he knew everything about my illness. Would I connect as well with another doctor? His resolve to get all the cancer was proven by the long twelve hours that he and his team had endured. He was not too proud to ask for help when he made the discovery of that much cancer. He didn't even stop for lunch and dinner; they fed him his meal through a straw. He stayed there all day and worked on me, cutting, scraping, and cleaning as he went. Here was a man who came out of a twelve-hour surgery to talk to my folks all bent over because his back was wrecked after the many hours of hunching over my body. His scrubs were bloody and soaked with sweat. The little green cap was pasted to his forehead as he was telling my parents that there was no chance. It was fatal. As he went into details of the surgery, it became very clear how badly off I was.

And yet, even as the words fell from his mouth, I believe there was doubt from him. He was saying those things because that was what the evidence indicated. All that cancer and the vast amounts of tissue, muscle, veins removal, and then the countless tumors had to lead us somewhere. He didn't want to give false hope. As the surgery indicated, there was little hope. Statistically, the odds were in favor of death. He wanted it known from the start. It wasn't a doom and gloom kind of thing, just facts. He made it very clear that only a few made it through when the odds were stacked against them like this. But he made the ultimate decision to save my arm.

He decided to scrape the cancer from my collarbone and then spent the hours meticulously picking the cancer from my vocal cords. He was sure that he could get it all. Would I speak again? Would I sing? That wasn't important. The question was, would I live? He thought so. This is why he spent twelve excruciating hours trying to repair me. Was he a believer? I don't think Dr. Schafer put on airs. He saw something that he thought he could fix, that all the hours of training would culminate into repair. The masked man had done his part. Was it just up to me to do the rest? No, it was up to God and the storm of prayers.

I had only met him a week prior to surgery. This was the same man who wrote on the green pad of paper that it was a matter of life and death. How did he know? I thought he was just saying that so I could get coverage. This was the same guy who smiled at me and said it was all going to be right, that there was nothing to worry about. This was the same guy who I would find sitting at a bar in Coronado, California, years later talking with friends and telling me he would never forget my case. It created an everlasting impression on him. This was my unmasked man. This was my Dr. Jeffrey Schafer.

4

The Stay

I CHECKED INTO THE HOSPITAL and began three days of heavy testing, which meant the kitchen sink. You name it, I had it—top, bottom, and middle. I think they even made some up so they could try it out on me! There was a 99.9 percent chance of it not being cancer, that it was an enlarged thyroid and a large growth on the side of my neck. Everyone was good with that. They scheduled the surgery for Friday around noon. He said it would last about two to two and a half hours.

I had a very bad feeling. I remember telling my mom that no matter what, "make sure they don't cut my arm off." First off, there was no they...well, at the time, there wasn't. How did I know there would be a bunch of doctors? Secondly, my mom said, "Lett, he is operating on your neck, not your arm." She later told me that I became very agitated about my arm and made her promise to tell the doctor no matter what. Thank God she did. The doctor thought she was nuts. He told her that they were operating on my neck. "Okay, thanks for telling me."

~Little White Pill Time~

It was almost time to go in. I was getting a bit worried. I had a sinking feeling in my stomach. My stomach had always been my warning beacon. It always tells me when something is about to happen. Good or bad, the warning always comes. I had a torch going off and away I went!

The nurse gave me a little pill to relax and calm me down. I swallowed the pill. Deb, my older sister, passed out. Splat! Right on the ground. The nurse made some comment about never having seen that kind of effect before. What happened was, my loving sister decided about two weeks prior that she was too heavy. She needed to go on a diet. Bam! No sugar, no fruit, or anything with sugar in it. When Deb came to, the nurse asked her a few questions. When she got to the part about eating, my sister divulged the fact that she hadn't eaten anything with sugar for two weeks. Well, that took all the pressure off me. Everyone immediately began to fuss over my sister.

My family—which consisted of my father, mother, sister, Ralph, my brother-in-law, and Joe Masar (not my brother, but my non-adopted brother)—were present. The first few hours were not too bad. I imagine they went and had coffee, talked a bit, and waited. You know, the standard stuff while waiting. Everything was okay until the first two hours became three, then four, and then five. No one came out to talk to them. No one even looked at them. They kept inquiring but everyone was busy. There was something weird going on. In the course of the four or five hours, my sister said she knew something was wrong. She overheard and saw an orderly ask where he should take the food for Dr. Schafer and his team. Deb said it was a large cart of food. Now this is where my family was trying not to panic.

When the surgery started, it was only Dr. Schafer. When did he get a team? In addition, why did he have a team? Better yet, a team for what? It was supposed to be a simple procedure. Now it was after 6:00 p.m. and I had already been in surgery for six hours. Moreover, apart from the fact that Deb saw the food cart and that there was now a team of doctors still in there with me, my folks still knew nothing. I can't imagine what my family was going through. After eight hours, they still had not heard a thing. I don't think they ate, went to the bathroom, or even left to drink water. At any moment, someone was sure to come out and tell them what was going on. Waiting with terror, thinking there must have been a mistake, the doctor had forgotten about them. Surely, I wasn't still in surgery.

Maybe they got started late because of an emergency, trying to reassure themselves that everything was all right. This went on for twelve excruciating hours. I know I went through it physically, but the pain my family felt that day must have been unbearable. Many rosaries were said that day.

5

The News

BLINK AND POOF, I'M DYING. My chance for survival .01%! I was a goner. Poor Dr. Schafer came creaking out from the double doors of the operating room. His back was killing him from being bent over me for twelve hours. This was the worst part of his job, telling parents that their daughter had extensive cancer. He labored so hard, he even brought in a team of other doctors. They did what they could. It was unbelievable. He had to tell them that I would most likely die that night!

That's all my mom could hear. She ran to the chapel and started praying and crying. Dr. Schafer told them to go in and say their goodbyes. Dr. Schafer was completely surprised when he opened me up. He thought he was going to find one large tumor on the side of my neck. What he found was a multitude of tumors stacked one on top of the other. There were so many tumors that they couldn't even adhere to whatever muscle tissue was still left. The cancer wrapped itself around my larynx and if I did live, I would never talk again.

Somehow within the first six hours, an incredible surgical team was put together. First, one doctor was called because a certain part of my neck was a concern, then another, and then another, and finally, a shoulder doctor was called. It was too incredible, none of the doctors left. They all stayed. The five doctors called in to assist were mesmerized. They had never seen anything like this. Spellbound, they couldn't move an inch from this astonishing case. They had to see how it was going to turn out!

Since I was young and strong, they all felt I had a good chance for survival. Still, the odds were stacked against me. Being twenty-five had its grace. I am not sure why they kept scraping and sewing after hours seven through twelve. They really should have stopped. They really should have cut my arm off, which would have made my prognosis better. They didn't even reach my arm until hour seven. What took most of the time was the use of the dental pick on my throat. They took turns picking the cancer off my larynx.

After twelve hours, they still hadn't finished. I still had cancer on the right side of my neck, but my body was dying. I was going into shock so they had to stop. There was a heart pack ready should it be needed. There was never time for any form of reconstructive surgery either. They would tend to that later. So they put back everything they could save and closed me up. I had a large dent on the left side of my neck because they had to take all the affected muscle tissue out with the cancer. The team wasn't too worried about how they put me back together, just that I got back together before I died.

I didn't get a transfusion because my body was too weak. A weak body makes a perfect breeding ground for a deadly infection. This would cause a major problem post-surgery. There was so much cancer that they didn't even need a pathology report. That would be used later on to find clean margins, which means that the cancer had not spread further. This was good and bad. Good because the doctors could easily see the cancer and remove it, not wasting any time; bad because there was so much and it was taking a very long time. I'm sure they kept thinking the surgery was going to end, but they just kept on finding more and more cancer so no fresh blood for me. Later, I would recycle my own blood! A second surgery would have to be scheduled if I made it and if I was strong enough to endure another major surgery.

The good news is Dr. Schafer thought he knew what they were up against the second time. I do remember Dr. Schafer showing me how far the second incision would go with a hand mirror. He also told me that as I grew older, the scar would blend in to the natural folds of my neck. He was correct about the scar on the right side. I'm in my sixties now, and it does blend in okay but the left side just had too much of everything missing. The large "dent" is still there and looking more like an ancient sagging valley.

Dr. Schafer then told my family that if my mom had not asked him to save my arm, he would have instructed the other doctor to cut it off. The cancer had gone all the way to tip of my shoulder. They literally scraped me to the bone. What they did is called a radical, which means they took out all the muscles, lymph nodes, nerves, and whatever else to get the cancer. It is a very drastic surgery. They did this by making a large incision from behind my left ear to the bottom of my collarbone, then down across my neck about eight inches. It looked like they almost cut my head off. The skin was stretched and folded open so that a piece rested on my chin area and the other piece lay over my shoulder. Much later when I could talk, I asked the doctor how they did that. He looked surprised and asked who had told me. I told him I just saw it.

People talk about out-of-body experiences all the time. I tried to explain it in the beginning of the book. It's a very weird experience, hard to believe, and even harder to explain. Back in the seventies, this was unheard of. He persisted, claiming that someone must have told me. I assured him that I saw it. I do remember floating around the operating room and watching. I was not grossed out by any of what I was seeing. I knew it was my body, but it really didn't matter. It was all so interesting seeing my neck muscles exposed. There were so many colors and I looked just like something you would see in a medical book. There really was no way I could have known how they stretched my skin.

Clinically, the left shoulder girdle muscles, thyroid gland, the left ancillary lymph nodes, and left exterior jugular vein had all been removed. They cut from the hyoid bone to the sternal notch and had to reattach the veins with multiple bypasses. It was that big of a mess. The cancer was entangled all around the nerves and muscles! The thyroid was completely engulfed with cancer. It was a wonder I wasn't a lunatic from the lack of a functioning thyroid. The bottom left parathyroid gland was removed; the other three lobes were salvaged but questionable. It was during the surgery that they froze one of my vocal cords. If I lived, then maybe I would be able to make a sound for others to understand. The doctor who thought they should cut my arm off then scraped most of the muscle off of my collarbone all the way down to the tip of my left shoulder blade.

Since I messed up the first plan for my surgery, a new one had to be developed very quickly. It was very lucky for me that I wasn't older or they would have taken one look at the extensive cancer and muscle damage and then closed me back up. It looked pretty grim. There was just too much cancer. But as we know, doctors are in the business of hope and healing.

6

Morphine

BACK IN THE SEVENTIES, MORPHINE was regarded as the gold standard of analgesics used to relieve severe or agonizing pain and suffering. Knowledge is power. Man, I wish I knew that. I thought you got hooked right away and became an instant drug addict, wiping out my teaching career before it started. I could just see me on skid row, homeless and sniffling (drug addicts do that sniffling thing) and begging for money to get my next fix, just like on TV. I was scared. I wanted off this stuff. It was going to grab me and never let me go! I already developed track marks on both arms to prove it. There was no place to go but down!

While in the ICU and then in the first few days of my regular room, I was still "on the stuff, man." They had to keep me still and quiet. The pain was agonizing even with the morphine. Muscle tissue had been scraped to the bone; muscles were now missing; and my body had been poked, prodded, ripped apart, and sewn back together very quickly. In some spots, it was a beautiful straight line halfway across my neck; in others, wiggly might describe it. Lumpy and bumpy or swollen and red is another description. I still needed at least one more surgery. Good God! What would that look like? How was I ever going to get off these drugs? Would I need to get a trench coat and oversized thigh boots when I went to live in the alleyway?

On more than two occasions, I recall the effects of the drugs. I remember feeling light and invincible. Morphine also relieves fear and anxiety by producing a sense of euphoria with the release of endorphins. It also impairs physical and mental performance, such as the simple task of brushing my teeth. I understand why people get hooked on this stuff. It feels great, it really does. I recollect one time just after they had put the shot in my IV bag while I was lying flat on my back. I could feel the effects of the drug starting to course through my veins. It was a warm, calming sensation. Everything stopped. I could hear the hands on the clock tick. I felt good, happy, and peaceful. No pain. I closed my eyes. Then I realized, *I'm on drugs! Ooh, so this is what it's like. Ah, okay. Let's see what I can do. Ah-huh! Foot, move!* I commanded. Nothing. *Move, foot,* I repeated. Waiting for something to happen, my hand moved, I giggled. *Hand, move.* My foot moved. I giggled again. I started telling myself to move different parts of my body only to find that my body had a mind of its own. *Oooh, drugs. I'm trippin' out, man! Hey, look at my hand. It's so big! I'm on drugs! Oooh!* I croak out in my best whisper, "Debbie, Debbie, watch this". I make a command to my body and some other part moves. We giggled.

She then asked the nurse how long I would be like that and was assured that it was just the initial effect. I would go to sleep soon enough. She was right, but wow, what a feeling! I will never forget that awesome but terrifying feeling. After a while, they started to wean me off the drugs as per my request. I needed to teach, not be a drug addict. I begged them. I was a baby and cried, shaking my head, "No, no, I don't want it!" Everything made me cry then. I think that was the drugs too. They wanted to keep me calm and still; I wanted off the drugs! I finally got some other opiate. I just didn't know it was an opiate, and it was just as addictive. It was always placed through the IV because I couldn't swallow anything as large as a pill. It would be weeks before I took a pill orally. I was now sitting and walking a bit. I was still on IV and had a few other things attached, but I was grateful that I had a cute, little froggy voice. I could sit in a chair and not be in bed.

My left arm was getting stronger. Everyone was very encouraged. They needed to test my left arm to see what it could do and assess the damage. My arm was a vegetable, it just laid there like a big zucchini. In order to move it, I needed to pick it up with my right hand. When I let go, it dropped like a sack of potatoes. Thud! I just couldn't seem to control the heavy weight of my left arm. It was as if my mind and my arm were not talking to each other. My fingers and hands were working. I could hold things and move my wrist and my elbow a little. I just couldn't lift it. Dead weight! I didn't get it. Why would this affect my arm? Literally, my arm and my brain were not speaking to each other. The reason was simple. The muscle for lifting and controlling the weight of the arm was partially cut out. When the doctors made the decision to save my arm, they had to dissect part of the muscle tissue, scrape around the bone, and then hope for the best. With all that surgery and exploration, my entire shoulder area had taken a direct hit. It was swollen and very sensitive, and muscle tissue was MIA.

However, things were looking up. I spoke in a low range with little volume, somewhere between a whisper and a sexy Kathleen Turner rasp. But that too was getting better daily. The cute physical therapist was going to conduct a few tests to see what was going on between my brain and my arm. Did I mention he was cute? I was twenty-five, you know. He instructed me to close my eyes then told me he was going to place a few objects in my left hand to see if I can distinguish what they were. He covered my eyes with a towel over my head so I wouldn't peek. *Foolish, I look foolish!*

"Ready?" he said.

Cool, I'm on drugs, baby. Bring it on! He placed a ballpoint pen in my hand. *Wait, I know this! It's something you write with. A netting needle? A knitting needle? No, wait…a pencil. Uh, oh, a pen! Yeah, I got it right! This was fun! Do another one.* He placed something else my hand. *Okay, okay. It's long, heavy, and pointy. It has a flat side and a pointy side.* Poke! *Ouch! Did that hurt? Yes, I think it did. Wait, wait, I know this too.* I was giggling a little. *A nail, a nail, a big fat nail!* "A nail!" I croaked.

What? I got it wrong? How come? It felt like a nail. Why wasn't it a nail? It should be a nail. I ripped the towel off. I looked at it and saw a straight pin. I was completely disappointed. *It really should have been a nail.* I just couldn't get my mind around the fact that it wasn't a nail. I was kind of getting sad. It really did feel like a nail! It was then that my sister stopped the test and told the guy that I had just been given my morphine and that this probably wasn't the best time for the test. He concurred, shook his head, and smiled. Then he left. We giggled. Then I slept.

7

The Last Rites

I RECEIVED THE ANOINTING OF the sick—or, as it was then called, the last rites—twice, once in ICU and then again just before the second surgery. I don't remember the first time or know if there are rules about how many times you can get it.

My mom says that Father Kulleck came in while I was in the ICU. She, my dad, and my sister were there too. The priest saw me, immediately put his stuff down, and started the rite. He didn't say anything to the family, just got busy, finished, and left. They were upset. "Did Father Kulleck just give our daughter her last rites?" In retrospect, that was typical Fr. Kulleck. He was a man of few words; no explanation, just action. He saw my need, knew my faith in God, then administered the rite. No questions, no discussion. It had to be done before I died so he just did it! My parents were shocked to realize I was in imminent danger of dying right then and there! For a priest to come barging in and administer the last rites without discussion was just crazy, unheard of, and never done before. How quick would it be? How much time would they have left with their daughter? Would I make it through the next hour, the night, or the next day? They needed someone to tell them what was going on!

In 1978, when one received this sacrament, you had to be actively dying. Not just really, really sick. If you were on your way out, it was a very big deal to receive this sacrament. It's not like it is now. Calling a priest to the hospital was huge in and of itself, but to call them in for the last rites was monumental! When this happened, everyone was miserable because usually after receiving the rite, the person would die. Sometimes they would even die during the rite. In either case, death was inevitable. Whenever we heard of someone getting the rite, we would be heartbroken because we knew it wouldn't be long until they died. When someone received this, it was for real, for keeps, and forever. There was never an "Oops! Sorry, it's a mistake. She's really not dying." It was a grave, very serious matter, not one a priest took lightly. The priest had to go into the church, head to the special place where the holy oils were kept, and put them in a designated black box. This box had a crucifix, the oils, a special container for the Eucharist, and a special cloth to catch any bits of Eucharist or oil that might fall. He also had his stole and brought along his personal prayer book.

Just to kill this point, you understand how it was then. Prior to that, we never even saw the holy oils, let alone knew where they were kept! If they did use them, the priest had to make sure the person was really dying. Not close or may recover; but death, dying, gone, or not coming back. I was there in all respects. Good-bye. See you in heaven. This is what my family and friends were going through. That last bit of earthly connection before I was gone, the last breath, the last sign, and then I'd be gone from them forever.

As I write this, it is hard to believe that I was that close to death. It doesn't seem real. For me, it only redefined the fact that God did have a purpose for me on earth, that my job was not done, and that I still had too much to do. I don't remember any of part of the first anointing but I do remember parts of the second time. I had made it out of the woods only to get lost again. For my poor folks, going through that once must have been excruciating. I can't even imagine them watching me be wheeled away for a second time. My mom said that she knew a piece of her had been wheeled away that day. It was unbearable for these faith-filled people. It still hurts even if God is with you a hundred percent of the way.

~Anointing of the Sick~

What I do remember from that day is the way the holy oil smelled. It always takes me back every Easter Vigil when the holy oils are brought out and the new Catholics receive the oil. It is that essence that wafts through the church as they are being blessed, a smell that will always take me back to the hospital that day. It is one of the best fragrances in the whole world! Even though it takes me back to my sickest days, the way it makes me feel is extraordinary. Even now, I feel the presence of Christ deep within me. It's a feeling you never really want to let go of. If you've had it, you know. If you haven't well, you should check it out. Now I am not saying you should get sick to get it. What I mean is that once a year, the church has a mass for the ill, and they use the holy oil. There are healing masses and healing services. When I say you should go check it out, what I really mean is, do not hesitate to receive this wonderful sacrament. It may or may not heal you (only God will know the reason for that), but what it will do is soothe and smooth you, kind of like taking a wrinkle out. It will help put peace in your heart like nothing else can. It's that glorious feeling of awe enveloping your mind, heart, and soul. It's just like submerging your tired, weary body in to a hot bath. It's that release, that deep sigh of fulfilment. You are melting, and your cares just float away.

This sacrament may be received by people suffering from all kinds of serious or chronic illnesses, whether physical or mental. It is no longer given just for the dying. It is for the restoration of mind and body, a way to obtain that peaceful heart in such a powerful way.

As I was lying on my bed, the anointing of the sick went something like this. I was in my regular room with my family all around me. Father put all the tools he needed to administer the rite on the rolling food tray: his prayer book, his stole, the oils, holy water, a container for the consecrated Host, a crucifix, and a special cloth. There may even be a candle, depending on the safety factor. It is like setting up for the last spiritual meal, ridding yourself of any final sins you may have, and receiving the final gift of peace.

~The Rite Itself~

First, the rite begins with the sign of the cross with blessed water, which reminds us of our baptismal promise to die with Christ so that we might rise to new life with Him. I remember how cool and refreshing the water felt on my skin. Father did not douse me with the water. He simply put it on my forehead in the sign of the cross and put it on my upturned palms. I was open and ready to receive anything that was coming my way. Tears were in my eyes as I started to breathe a little heavier. I remember my mom getting a little concerned about that so I tried to stay calm. I can still see myself in the bed with sheets turned down and my arms resting above the sheets. I can't recall if I had an IV or anything, I just remember seeing how white the sheets were. I immediately started to feel His presence. It was amazing! I knew I was going to receive something special, but I was also very tired and kind of wanted to sleep too.

Next, readings from Scripture are adapted to the condition of the sick person. The priest prays and assures the sick person of the prayers of the parish and invites the sick person to pray for the needs of his or her fellow parishioners. I must have dozed off here because I do recall a murmur or a soft, rhythmic voice. I was just completely comfortable and so relaxed.

Then the priest imposes hands on the head of the one to be anointed, prays over the oil, and anoints the forehead and hands of the sick person. The hands! Yes, the hands, heavy and gentle at the same time. Father placed them on my forehead. It was at that moment that I knew it was all right. Did that mean I was going to live? Was I going to die? It didn't matter. Nothing mattered at that time. Peace. Stillness. It was going to be all right. That's all I knew. Others placed their hands on me. I was floating, comfortable, breathing softly and gently, no longer in the hospital. It's hard to explain the feeling that washes over you. It is such a feeling of wellbeing. Again, nothing matters.

After that, the priest prays for the sick person and invites all present to pray the Lord's Prayer. I heard many voices. I think I mouthed the prayer too. I am really out of it, sort of in a dream state. I was there but not there, aware of what was happening but very content not to participate. I could see Father moving stuff back and forth on the little table. He was very busy. *Why was he so busy?* Next, Holy Communion may be received at this time. I wish I could remember all of it. I felt good, quiet, and still. I don't remember anything hurting at that time. I didn't have communion as I was getting ready for the second surgery. You can't eat anything, even communion. I sleep peacefully. Finally, the priest then blesses the sick person and all present. I am sound asleep.

It was a pretty grim situation. My poor parents must have been beside themselves, yet again! At this anointing, my parents were fully present. They understood the full gravity of the situation. Watching and participating in this sacrament was their final act of love and preparation. I received the final blessing. I was dozing in and out of the rite, wondering why it took so long but still feeling good.

After the rite was over, I fell into a deep calm and restful sleep; not the kind I had been having, but very different. If I could, I would have turned to my side, placed my hands under my pillow and pulled the sheet to my chin. I was so comfortable, nothing hurt so I was good. It was okay. Whatever was going to happen, was going to be all right. Nothing mattered, not anymore. I was fine. No, I was more than fine. My mom said I had a warm, peaceful, and almost glowing presence. Words really can't do it justice. I won't say I was resigned to die. I really didn't think about it much. It just didn't seem to matter anymore. I closed my eyes and slept a profound, wonderful, and deep sleep.

8

Prayer

Vatican II was still very, very new; so was the concept of ecumenism, which was to promote unity and knowledge of other Christian faiths. Our church was and is still figuring out all the ins and outs of this monumental document. But in my hospital room, it was flourishing. Literally and truly a parade. At least one person of every faith had been by my room and prayed with, on, and over me. In the beginning, it was just my own personal faith. The Catholic priest from my parish, and the chaplain from the hospital would come by to visit. Sometimes they would stay for a while, chatting with my family, reading from the Bible, or saying special prayers, and there was always a blessing. I had a lot of visitors. I am not sure how it happened that so many different faiths came to my room. There was only one sign on my door, "Limit your visits to five minutes." Nothing like "All faiths welcome. Come on in and pray a spell." I knew the four W's: the who (prayer leaders from many different faith groups), the what (prayers raining down on me), the where (my hospital room), and the when (in God's time), but equally as important was the how (being open to prayer regardless of Christian denomination). That was my parents' doing, their love of Christ and their openness to prayer.

My first recollection of this was when I had moved to a regular room. I would open my eyes from sleeping (or just "zoning") and there would be a priest praying over me. Then I would go back to sleep and wake again only to see a preacher-type person praying over me. I knew they were pastors because they, unlike Catholic priests, carried a Bible. A Catholic priest always had their special little black prayer book and a stole. Plus—the real give away—a priest always wore a black shirt and a white collar, but because it was the seventies, the preacher man always wore a pastel shirt with his collar. I think the drugs had something to with my color perception! Many times, I would see all these different people praying over me. They were Catholic, Methodist, Lutheran, and Baptist. When they heard that the room down the hall was accepting prayers, they came out of the woodwork. A couple of times, people would stand around my bed, lay their hands on me, and pray.

Laying on of hands came from the time of Jesus. There are hundreds of references in the Bible of Jesus healing people this way. The apostles were given the gift of healing through the laying on of hands. It is something Protestants practice and believe in. It was not something the seventies Catholic did! The priest would do it sometimes but we were not used to being "prayed on." Period. This was a big deal and very foreign to us all. My mom and dad let it happen because they were open to prayer. They just figured it was the Protestant way. What was weird was I always felt like I was floating. When they laid hands on me, it always gave me the most peace. Wrapped in this blanket of protective stillness, a calm serenity washed over me. I felt like I was being held in His arms, that nothing was going to happen to me. It was one of the best sensations ever. I loved it then and still do when people pray on me. My mother would say that when they prayed over me, I would radiate His peace; that even though I looked as terrible as I did, no one saw that, they just saw Christ. They would leave my room crying not because I was dying, but because they felt it. These were very profound moments in Christ. Again, drugs or prayer? You decide. I know my answer. No, not drugs, but the power of prayer!

~The Prayer Wheel~

Our parish of St. Pius X wasn't that big. Everybody basically knew everyone. I had been leading, singing, and playing the guitar in the choir plus doing weddings, funerals, and special occasions for years. I was a face there, people knew me. Even while I was living in South America, people prayed for my safe return. Around the same time, two other tragedies had befallen our little parish. Kevin was diagnosed with a brain tumor and Mike had been in a terrible accident in which two thirds of his body was burned. All three of us were in our twenties, and none of us were expected to survive.

When the word got back to St. Pius that I made it through the first night after surgery but was still very grave, my little church catapulted into action. A prayer wheel was started. A group of believers: my mom, my dad, Kevin's and Mike's folks, the Fetters, Doris, and a few other wonderful friends gathered every Monday to pray for the sick, injured, and anyone who may need prayer. This little but mighty group had witnessed many miracles. Countless times, the group would be praying for hopeless causes, likes ours, and miracles would occur. These humble people never took credit for God's work. They never said, "Look what we did"! They were simply faithful, strong, and loving people.

A prayer wheel is an old-fashion method of communication, before technology. The word had to get out. Names were put on sheets of paper and passed out. One person called the next person and on and on until it circled back to the first person, thus creating the circle part of the prayer wheel. St. Pius never incorporated this method before, but action had to happen and it had to happen fast! A new bond of urgency was bringing our community together and living the life of grace through prayer to journey together with a fresh purpose and a renewed climate for St. Pius. They were becoming a living witness of action and love.

There was a core of my parents' friends who decided that a rosary must be held that night. I was critical, near death and needed a tremendous amount of prayers. They began to contact people. It spread like wildfire and exceeded all expectations. The church was packed. It was and still is amazing to me how such a monumental task could have taken place without the Internet. I now know that through their belief and dedication, the Holy Spirit guided their prayers at St. Pius that night. As Pops Leonard said, "Let us bombard the heavens with our prayer!" It truly was an explosion of prayers to heaven, and God heard it. They were relentless. They never stopped prayer the entire time I was in the hospital! The crowds remained steady at church. They all received reports of my progress and how their prayers were making a difference. They also realized that if it was God's will for me to die, so be it. I would be with God. What better reward for my hard battle. The group not only prayed for the three of us, but for our families and close friends' peace and understanding of God's will. With their prayers for us came a most wondrous thing by being the vessel for the Holy Spirit. His love cascaded through them, filling their hearts with overwhelming grace. All the while, the same core of friends came and sat with my folks in the hospital. They would pray for them, bring them meals, or just be with them. These prayer warriors were the ultimate support my family needed. They were "Christ with skin on."

~The Gift of Faith through the US Postal Service~

I'm finally home after my last surgery. I can't wait to get to my bedroom and collapse on my bed. *Okay, maybe I'll need a little help.* It was so good to be home. I was on my bed with my own pillow! I look like a mummy with all the bandages around my neck, but I didn't care. I was home! I don't think it had been more than five minutes and I was sound asleep.

When I woke from my nap, I remember looking around my bedroom, enjoying the familiarity and comfort it gave me. Then my eyes settled on my closet door. It was a large, double-door closet, plastered from top to bottom without an inch to spare with cards and letters. As my eyes swept across the doors, reaching the bottom I saw four grocery bags heaping full of cards and letters.

What's all this? There is just so much of it. Why am I crying? It hit me. It was love in a bag, full of faith and trust. My mom displayed the cards so I could see and feel them at all times. Hundreds of people took time to write me their prayers, wishes, and thoughts. There were cards from every state, even Canada, Mexico, and

Europe. Some of my parents' friends went to Rome and sent a few postcards to my parents, saying that they were praying for us in our time of need. So, that counts, right?

This simple action of writing and mailing a card became a sea of love, support, trust, and faith, not just for me, but also for my family and close friends. They knew that they were not alone, that God was with them at all times, and that his earthly angels fly to the mailbox to prove it!

Mom had given me a little bell to ring in case I needed anything, plus, she didn't want me to strain my voice. I rang it. "Mom, can you get me one of those bags of cards?" She smiled but didn't say a word, reached over gave it to me, kissed my head, and left quietly.

I shook my head slightly, marveling at the grace of my mom and then eagerly reached in to read a few. "We love you...We are praying for your full recovery...Hope to see and hear you singing in church soon...We miss you." *Who are these people? I don't even recognize their names? How could they pray for me, they don't even know me!* My chest was a little tight (in a good way) because a sea of support and love had just washed over me. Now I'm overwhelmed and crying again. These people were fulfilling their mission in the world. They were answering their call to action and showing their faith in God. These are the modern-day signs of miracles. A postage stamp by itself is not miraculous but what it brings and the comfort it provides is. The senders all knew that their prayers could make a difference. *Oh my god, they are sending me their love and trust and I can feel it!* I fell gently asleep with card in hand and letters spilled across the bed.

I know in my heart I am a living witness, a living testimony to prayer. All three of us survived. Kevin is living strong. Mike recovered from his burns and is doing well. All three of us were dying. All three of us were given last rites. Our parents were all told to say goodbye to their children. But, through their prayers, they learned how to give their children back to God, knowing all the while that their wishes for their children to stay with them may not be God's will. That's the hardest part. How does anyone do that? When we pray and don't receive the answer we want yet we still believe and trust. That is true faith!

I do believe that God heard all the praying from my family, friends, and strangers. This is one reason God has kept me here. How wonderful for me to know this. I am to spread the word of prayer. My journey gives hope. This is very humbling to realize. I should have died, yet I lived. I truly believe it was through the grace of God and the thunder of prayers that showered the heavens in my name, that it was not my time, feeble as that may sound. Even now after all these years, I don't think I will ever absorb the enormity of it all. Me, who am I? For this reason, I never hesitate or hold back from talking about my cancer and my faith. I share my story because God didn't hesitate or hold back anything for me.

This transformation did not come right away. It took many years to develop. At first, it was me sharing with people who had cancer one on one. Later, it grew to small and large groups of people. That's why I am here. I am far from perfect. I mess up all the time. Every day, I try to be the light of Christ, to be that walking testimony that he entrusted me to be but I forget. Life gets in my way. I just keep trying. That's all He wants, not to give up and to trust Him. I am a walking, living, and breathing miracle of God. All hope should have been lost but here I am.

9

The Weight of Waiting

GOD HAS ALWAYS BEEN THE most profound presence in my mother's life. From her first waking moment to her last sleepy breath at night, God began and ended her day. He was her rock and salvation. Nothing—and I mean nothing—was done without consulting God. Now she found herself smack-dab facing her daughter's death. Suddenly, this became the ultimate test of her faith.

Her friend Ray Herman kept telling her to "Give Letty to God." She told me this many times. She was petrified. She just knew if she did, God would take me home. She didn't want that. She wanted me here with her, well and strong. When she would go to the prayer service, she would pray for my recovery, but not give me to God. Although she knew Ray was right and that was the only way, how could she relinquish me to God? Time after time, mom would step into church, pray intensely for my recovery, but not hand me to God. She just couldn't go that deep, it was too big of a sacrifice.

It was then that story of Abraham came to mind; only for mom, it was her daughter. They both had to surrender their children to God. Abraham waited over a hundred years for his boy. Mom had to stay in bed for the first six months in order for her body to keep me. Bedrest to save your unborn child is sane, but sacrificing your kid? I think Abraham might have been nuts! She didn't want to go where her prayers were taking her. This action was going against the "mother credo." Abraham was willing to take the knife in his hand and give up his son to God. Was my mother? How could she give up her Letty? How did Abraham do it? "God help me, I'm so weak!" She began to cry.

If it meant that I was to die, would her trust in God be violated? I don't think so because we believe in our afterlife with Christ. Mom knew I would be released from my painful burden here on earth.

Finally, she knew she had to do it. It was early in the morning before she went to the hospital. There are many, many questions. Could she do it? He really might take me home. Was she strong enough to endure this kind of pain? Would she feel guilty if I died because she gave me up? Was it giving up on her daughter or giving in to God's will? Was her faith strong enough to pull her through?

I was in intensive care when my dad needed to catch up on things at work. It had been an excruciating week, so many ups and downs, but I was still with them. I had already beaten the odds in so many ways. The time had finally come for her to go to St. Pius. For some reason, she parked in front of the church. The site was so familiar to her. She had been there while they constructed the church. She remembered them putting in the landscape and the multiple steps. They even put a small landing between the two flights to break it up and give the climbers a rest. Now it seemed to her that she was climbing Mount Everest. Each step took so much effort. Her feet had bricks attached to them. Her heart was pounding; her breath staggered.

Was it chilly? No, it shouldn't be. It was summer. Blessed mother. She shivered and looked up just a few more steps. *Breathe.* She remembered her favorite prayer. She began automatically. **Remember, O most gracious Virgin Mary.** She thought, *I don't remember the doors being this large and heavy.* She got to the doors, hesitated, took another deep breath, yanked on the door, and thought, *When did the door get so heavy?* She walked in. The aroma of beeswax, wood polish, and Christ enveloped her. She sees the first pew in the last row and plops down. She feels the comforting curve of the bench, familiar and smooth. Her eyes drifted to the kneeler. She looked up to the altar. *Gosh, it hadn't been that long since they had moved the altar to the front of the sanctuary.* She sighed and fixed her gaze on the red glow of the candle next to the tabernacle. Her eyes swept across the front of the sanctuary, from left to right. She sees Jesus with His palms open wide, Mary in blue and white, and the joyful statue of St. Pius with his little cap, all waiting as racks of candles burn nearby. A feeling of warmth and peace brushed her briefly.

Should she go to the statue of Jesus or go to the altar? Mary? Her knees were weak. She wanted to sit right where she was. She stood, feeling like her heart was being ripped out. She continued the longest mile straight down the middle of the church right in front of the altar. She stopped and waited. It was quiet, not a sound, except for her ragged breathing. She got to the sanctuary, and her attention was drawn to the tabernacle. This is a bold move on my mom's part for prior to the seventies, few were ever allowed to be in the sanctuary, which is a most sacred place. The pull to this area was forcibly strong. This was where she had to lay me down. Summoning all her courage, she timidly took her first step, crossing the area where the communion rail had once been. She could hardly breathe under the tidal wave of emotions bombarding her. Her knees couldn't support her, they buckled. She collapsed into a crumpled heap, sobbing. The tears flowed as if I was already dead and gone from her forever.

How can I do this? How can I give her to you? Her lungs burned. She was wracked with pain. *I must…*

She continued, deep in prayer, **"…that never was it known that anyone who fled to your protection, implored your help or sought your intersession was left unaided. Inspired by this confidence, I fly to you…"**

She wept, **"… in your mercy hear and answer me…"**

My mother was feeling like Mary, watching her Son go to the cross and knowing she couldn't do anything about it. She then relinquished her own desire to the will of God. *Heavenly Father, she is yours, she was never mine. You lent her to me.* Through her tears, she continued. *I thank you for this gift.* She stopped, knowing what she must say. *I release my Letty to you, dear Lord. Your will be done. I trust you, Lord!* With one last sob, a profound burst of jagged air was expelled. She leaned back, sitting, not as wrinkled, no longer in a heap, fewer tears, less sorrow. She was drained. I can't even imagine how she felt, telling God to go ahead take me if He must. "I believe. I trust. She is yours."

What faith! She had done it! My faith-filled mother surrendered. My mom said that after leaving the church, it was as if a huge weight had been lifted from her shoulders. She felt that she could breathe again. She really hadn't noticed that her chest had been tight and that her breathing had been shallow until she walked out of the church. Fresh air, a deep cleansing breath. *It felt so good.* Another, deep breath. "*Oh my Lord, thank you. It feels good. My Letty is yours.*"

The outcome was still very unsure, at least by the doctor's standard. But my mom knew that whatever happened was God's will. It was going to be all right.

10

Mouth Scum and Grape Juice

THE WEEKS HAVE MELTED TOGETHER. I am stronger now, and I am in a regular room with regular nurses. What did that mean? Could I try to eat, maybe get up, or wash my hair? No, not yet. Have visitors? Just a few. Stay awake for more than ten minutes? Okay, well, maybe five. Take a shower? No to that too! Brush my teeth? Soon, very soon. Wow, I am getting better! I remember waking up one time and seeing the tracheotomy and heart packs leaning on the wall within reach behind the blood-recycling machine. I thought, *Wow, someone must be really sick around here!* Did I mention I was the only one in the room? Ah, the drugs were still working their magic!

When I was moved to a regular room, the recycler came with me. We had "grown" together. I felt disgusting. I hadn't showered in weeks so I smelled like Betadine, and my hair was gross (*Ugh!*). Many things had to transpire before I got permission to have my hair washed. First, I had to get the drains pulled, which meant no more recycling machine. Also, I had to get off the oxygen, be able to sit, then walk a few steps, go to the bathroom, eat solid food and keep it down, and then finally, brush my teeth. That's all. But slow and steady just like the little train that thought he could, I was really getting stronger daily.

It's the day. My first food in what felt like weeks. Wow, that almost sounds like I am a baby getting her first solid food! Alas, it was not to be solid. *What? Grape juice? I get grape juice, that's it? No food? Okay, one step at a time.* It smelled so good that it made my mouth water. It had been a long time since I had eaten anything that didn't come from a bottle or a through the IV!

What happens to a mouth if one doesn't talk, eat, or get to brush? All those things help keep plaque from forming in your mouth. I hadn't been eating and just now starting to drink water from a straw. My talking was a low, quiet whisper, thus not creating much saliva. I still hadn't been given permission to brush my teeth just because it still required too much energy, and I was still pretty weak. All of a sudden, I was aware of my mouth. I hadn't noticed anything wrong with it before. I just wet my cracked lips with my moss-covered tongue when, *Oh no, my lips, my tongue. What?*

Imagine, if you will, a mouth cracked and dried, covered with slivers of dry, broken flesh. It actually felt like I had a balloon wrapped around my tongue…well, not a balloon because that would be smooth. It was more like sock, only wet and foreign. Feeling across my teeth, they seemed slimy and thick. My gums were buried in a mire of alien sludge. It didn't feel like my mouth.

What was happening? Did the cancer go to my mouth? Was this what cancer in the mouth felt like? How had the cancer gone to my mouth so quickly? It was everywhere! It was as if green pond scum had filled my mouth. It felt like that same film I would pick up on a stick as I played at a stagnate pond as a child, that same scum that my mom told me to stay away from. That was in my mouth now! *Why had I not noticed it before? What was this stuff?* I could peel it off. *Ugh!* It was all over my teeth, my gums, and my tongue! *Help, I was drowning in gack!* I couldn't even think of drinking grape juice with this stuff in my mouth.

My eyes started to leak. That seemed to be the fallback emotion. I mastered the technique of expressing my feeling without getting overwrought. There was no fooling my mom who realized that I must stay calm if I wanted some juice. I whispered to the nurse, "Is this cancer in my mouth?"

"No, sweetie, just plaque. Remember, since your throat is still giving you trouble, you haven't been talking, eating, drinking, or swallowing much. When you don't do these things, plaque builds up." She assured me it wasn't cancer.

I'm fine. There was so much about my cancer that I didn't understand. We had been on survival mode and were just now beginning the healing phase. It would take me years to learn all the ins and outs of this cancer and how it had changed me forever.

The nurse gave me a moist towel and told me to wipe off the muck. Have you ever put a towel in your mouth? Then you know what I'm talking about. I didn't know what was worse, rubbing globs of gunk from my teeth on a towel or me gagging on the feel of that towel in my mouth while I wiped it off. The more I took off, the more there seemed to be. It was becoming my own science fiction movie. *Was it multiplying? Did the friction of the towel actually cause it to grow?* It clung to my gums and even filled in the little dents and crevices between my teeth. It was grayish white, slippery and slimy. Really gross stuff. It came off in flat chunks as I peeled it off my teeth. It was harder to get it off my gums. My mom wet another washcloth as I continued to clean. I didn't get it all. I took a sip of water and choked or gagged a little. She then gave me ice chips. We were both gagging.

I am not sure why but I was always telling everyone that my mouth was hot. When I placed the chips in my mouth, they would melt very quickly. Swallowing ice chips this way allowed a very small trickle of liquid to slide down my throat. This was what the doctor had instructed us to do. The ice chips were cool and would help reduce the swelling in my throat, which was causing the entire problem. Oh yes, I also swallowed some of the slime chunks. Oh, and my mom later told me that my teeth had taken on multiple tones of gray. Repulsive! *Hmm, do you think I had bad breath?* I was spent. I needed to rest before I drank anything.

~Death by Grape Juice~

One full hour later, I awoke ready to have my first drink of real juice. I smelled the sweet nectar of the gods, as my dad would say! At long last, I am ready to drink. I moistened my lips with a smoother tongue. I took a drink. I swallowed. *Yum, tasty!* BAM! I started having a coughing fit. My throat was closing up, and I couldn't breathe. *There were bubbles in grape juice! Who knew?* The teeny tiny bubbles rubbed on the inner lining of my throat and felt like marbles being jammed down the pinhole opening of my esophagus. *Had I just swallowed a stick of dynamite that exploded down my throat?* I was drowning in grape juice as I clung to my last breath. *This was it, I'm dying!*

Simple cause and effect. *Next time you drink the stuff, take a closer look.* They aren't very big. One wouldn't think such tiny things would cause a problem but these particular bubbles caused a ruckus. Nurses, doctors, and family members all came running in. It was really quite chaotic in there. Everyone is trying to help me stop coughing. I am still hooked up to a ton of machines. The nurses are yelling, "Careful, careful! She might yank something out!"

That would have caused a new set of problems. Tears are streaming down my face. I couldn't stop coughing and I couldn't breathe. *Is this how it ends? On grape juice, really? I want my small bed! I can't believe that grape juice will be my demise.*

Away goes the juice and on goes the breathing mask. Straight up goes the bed, and my good arm is raised above my head while my useless left arm is hooked up to IV and meds. I am not giving birth but Lamaze breathing techniques are exercised. "Breath in, honey, and slowly breathe out. Try and calm down. Focus on the table. You're okay. All right, slowly breathe in." In all the excitement, I think the nurse was standing on the nasal breathing tubes, cutting off whatever oxygen I could get, making it impossible to inhale fully! It is really hard to suck in a breath when it feels like your lungs are pasted shut but I finally do calm my breathing and myself. Off comes the breather, tears are wiped away, face patted down from perspiration. *Whew, it's stopping! I'm okay. Breathe.* "Sip some water, Ms. Rocha." Okay, I did but just a tiny, tiny bit. *What if there were unknown bubbles in water?* Well, I had my first drink. I did it. Mouth scum and grape juice, what a morning! Success! I slept for the rest of the afternoon.

I would like to clarify the bubble ordeal. Simply put, my throat was very swollen. In addition, those grape juice bubbles had been too massive to pass without touching the inside passage of my throat, causing irritation and a coughing fit. Now in reality, most people don't even notice them. But I want you to understand just how small an opening I had in my throat. It was so swollen that those teeny tiny little bubbles caused havoc. It would be days later before I tried again. This time, they chose apple juice. It was wonderful, cool, refreshing, and sweet. The best part, no bubbles! I still can't drink grape juice today, but wine is good.

~Drain-oh~

The doctor and nurse told me I was getting off the recycling machine. Graduation day! The drain removal was really easy, they said. They just had to make sure everything was flowing correctly. They were going to pull the tubes. "Okay, brace yourself. This may pull a little."

A little? The tubes had grown into my flesh, forming a scab so when they pulled, I started to bleed. They kept pulling and it kept hurting. I mean, really, a lot! At first, it was just stuck as if the tube was part my skin. Then with a warm water compress and twisting and tugging, it started to give. Slowly it began to move. I could envision a snake with long fangs grabbing on to my stomach lining. I could feel the tail of the snake wiggling in me. *Yes, I am sure there was a snake in me now.* As they pulled, I thought I could feel my stomach being pulled through the tube. The snake's cold, pointy fangs gripping the lining of my stomach, unrelenting in its grasp. I begin to breathe rapidly. The pain is incredible. It had been one of the most painful things I had endured thus far. I was sure when they finished pulling the tube out, the snake would also come with my stomach attached to its teeth, just hanging there!

I am sweating, tears are leaking, and I am drugged out of my mind. *Huh, guess there was no snake in my stomach!* In a very weak, tiny little voice, I whispered, "Where's the snake?" Confused, the nurse and doctor looked at each other and gave one final tug. Luckily, I passed out from the pain. Thankfully they finished while I was asleep or unconscious or both!

.01%

~Brushy, Brushy~

The tubes are gone, and my teeth are beckoning to be cleaned! When I was finally allowed to brush my teeth, it felt like I had gone to heaven. What a wonderful feeling, all soft and not furry, squeaky clean, and no more white-gray slime. It did take some maneuvering. I had to have someone hold the basin while I spit because I only had one working hand. I was also uncoordinated. I had trouble getting the toothbrush to my mouth. Funny, I hadn't had brain surgery or had I?

What could have been a sad and tragic kind of thing was made lighter because of my sister. My sister was a godsend. She could make anyone laugh. This is one of her many gifts. Even as children, we would crack up because of something Debbie said or did. When she was in the eighth grade, she wore braces. She had tiny, cool, little circular rubber bands she had to wear. Each rubber band was connected to the top and bottom of her teeth. She was always flinging them from her mouth because she was laughing, making us laugh even harder because Deb was shooting rubber bands from her mouth. Losing my dexterity, my voice, and my life was dire. It's really not a time for laughter, but my family really doesn't follow the rules of protocol very much, especially when it comes to making a joke.

Scene one, Debbie enters. On my first attempt to brush my teeth, Deb handed me a small, odd-shaped little blue bowl. Then she handed me the toothpaste and the brush. Problem was, there were three things and I had only one hand to work with! Try as I might, I could not get my wet fish of a left hand to move up to the table. I grabbed it by the thumb and it would just plop on the table. There it sat. I then shoved the toothpaste in my left hand while unscrewing the cap with my right hand. I look at Deb. It's my turn to make her laugh. I spastically squeezed the tube. There must have been an air bubble in the tube because a pearl-sized drop squirted across the table, making a farting sound as it landed with a splat!

We started to giggle. It didn't help that my good hand somehow wasn't working perfectly either. Between the laughing and the brushing, I ended up looking like a rabid dog. It seemed that I was

59

also brushing my face and a little bit of my nose too. Drugs again? A little thing about laughing, it takes in air and air requires an opening in your throat. Neither of which I had. But that was okay, I had enough. My mom would scold Deb and try to get me to settle down because if I laughed too much, I would go into a coughing spell. Now laughter takes energy.

You may not think about what it takes to cough, but I did because it would always leave me spent. Coughing 101, coughing is nature's way of clearing our air passages of anything that irritates the throat and ends with the violent release of air we associate with a coughing sound. Did you read the part about violent? Anesthesia also causes mucus and sputum, gallons of it. If you start to cough that up, look out. These giant wads of sticky junk would get caught in my swollen throat. It was a very tricky thing to pass these globs and then catch my breath.

My whole body would react to coughing. It seemed every muscle in my body was affected, my stomach, my shoulders, and oh god, my neck! I haven't mentioned how many stitches I had. Let's just say there were tons, not a medical measurement. The stitches went across my neck from left shoulder to the midpoint of my right shoulder then down behind my left ear, meeting the longer incision. When I would go into this coughing spasm it was really quite something. Everyone was very nervous that I would spring a leak, pull a stitch, or pull something out. Keeping me calm was necessary. Every time I would graduate to a next step, it was monumental. Laughter, although wonderful and music to my parents' ears, had to be kept at bay. Too much was not a good thing, but some was okay. I finally got through my rabid dog teeth brushing challenge only to do my favorite thing. I fell asleep, exhausted from my latest adventure.

Progress was on the move in my room as I had mastered sitting on the edge of my bed, a chair, and standing while I held my IV pole. If you have ever drunk too much and had the spins, then you understand how standing felt to me at first. The tile in the floor kept moving, and I couldn't get my bearings. But I mastered that too. When I was allowed to sit on a chair as they changed the sheets, my legs would fall asleep. I would feel it start at my toes, go up through my ankles, and then stop around my knees. When the nurse would ask me to stand, I couldn't because I couldn't feel my legs. It would take several tries and a few people to maneuver my body and get me up. I was always hot, sweaty, and tired from the effort but grateful, just the same.

Walking to the bathroom was also fun. It was just so far away. Needless to say, I was very weak. My legs would also fall asleep while I sat on the toilet. Pulling the nurse call cord was hard because it was on my left side and my left arm wasn't working enough to pull it. I would have to reach over with my right hand and pull. A couple of times I fell off the toilet. What a spaz!

One time, my dad found me. I don't remember how long I stayed there. I was cold, shaking, and very shook up. I wasn't crying because by now, they had convinced me that crying was a bad thing. I couldn't call for help because my voice was still really weak. It was like a mini melodrama. Cue in old-timey piano. Who will save Letty from the bathroom floor? How long will she wait? Will the sun rise on the next day before she is found? After that episode, I had new nurses all of a sudden.

11

Knock, Knock, Who's There?

AT ONE TIME, THE NURSE told my mom that I had forty visitors waiting to come and see me while I was in intensive care. They were not allowed to come up so they all congregated downstairs in the waiting room. Joe and my family were the only people allowed up there. Sometimes Joe would just be sitting in the chair watching me. While in the ICU, I was heavily sedated. I needed to be still and not move. I couldn't talk so that was okay. I was tearing a lot, and my body temperature ran very hot. I was having a hard time getting back to a regular temperature. I did not have a fever but I was hot, I guess like a hot flash, only for days at a time not hours or minutes. Either my mom or someone would gently wipe the tears from my eyes and cool my face down a bit with a moist cloth. There is so little I remember from those days. When I finally did get into a regular room, it seemed I was inundated with love and people. My singing group had taken up camp in the outside waiting room. At times, they were so loud that the nurses had to either ask them to be quiet or to leave. They just wanted to be nearby.

My room had a revolving door. The thing your friends and family don't realize is that every person who walks through that door is robbing energy from the patient. They didn't mean to; they just wanted to see me, give their love, and show me they cared. But in the beginning, I was always left depleted. I could do nothing more than sleep. Even when I was in the regular room, I still slept a lot. Nevertheless, as time went on and I got stronger, the visits became more frequent. I can remember trying to keep my eyes open to visit my friends and relatives. I wanted to honor their visit by staying awake. I couldn't talk much so that's all I could do. However, my eyes would literally cross, and then I would be asleep only to wake to find a new pair of eyes staring at me. Oh, those eyes, those eyes! It took weeks to get all that blood and Betadine off me so my visitors were privy to my crusty appearance. While in the ICU, I had tubes and machines plugged in everywhere. Both arms had something inserted or attached. I think I had several finger clamps, a tube down my throat and one in my nose, the recycling machine, a heart sticker monitor and other monitor stickers, a catheter bag, and a few other assorted gizmos.

Making me presentable was not a priority for anyone. At one point, the veins in my arms gave way so they were using the veins in my ankles. My sister said it was painful just to look at me. I looked pitiful. At first, my dear friends and family couldn't get past the shock of my condition. You know when you see someone with a mole or zit on their nose, you don't want to stare but you can't keep your eyes from going there. Well, that's how it was. People kept talking to my neck. As I got better and time passed, I would remind people where my eyes were. Pointing to my eyes with two fingers, nonverbally insisting but not demanding, they meet me in the eyes and not at my scars. Unfortunately, this was becoming a well-practiced habit. Yeah, I'm sure I was real smooth about that too.

~The Rack~

Wow, what a marvel! Who wouldn't stare? It was fantastic. It was the newest machine for cleaning and filtering blood, and I got to use it. Every time I closed my eyes and then opened them again, the lifesaving, whirling metal wonder was there. I just couldn't resist watching the sight of my own blood circulating through this miraculous cleaner, which was looming over me. The only thing missing was Igor grinding the wheels of the medieval torture rack and me spilling my guts about the perils of grape juice and any other state secrets the men in white coats wanted.

The blood recycler held three vertically hinged boxes suspended on a rack by round metal pipes. They were about the size of two small shoeboxes, left and right, and a larger boot-sized box in the center (I love being a girl). There were a multitude of tubes coming from the smaller boxes implanted into my chest. The back and sides of the boxes were a white opaque plastic, and the front had a clear plastic sheet so you could see everything that was happening in the machine. The left side sucked the dark, gross blood out; the right side pushed the newly filtered blood back into my body. Everyone could see this thick, dark, maple syrupy blood going into the left box, swirl around, then go into the center box where it would be spun around again through wheels, filters, and more tubes, before propelling to the right box to emerge all thin, bright red, and healthy. Then my newly filtered, beautiful blood would pump down the tubes and back into a different set of chest tubes. I could imagine hearing the whoosh of air being sucked into the bellows in my torture chamber as Igor compresses the handles, forcing the air through the machine back into me. "She's alive! She lives!" Thank you, Igor!

I eventually got a floor-standing model, which brought down some of the interest because it wasn't hanging directly over me. *Did they have electricity in the middle ages? How come there are so many pretty lights?* I must be trippin' again.

~Those Staring Eyes~

Such sadness, such worried eyes, there was no way to communicate with anyone that I was going to be all right. At first, I really didn't think or do much; but as I got better, those eyes stayed the same. Such grief. My mom kept thinking that every time she left, she would never see me again. My sister said it just hurt so much to look at me. She couldn't imagine how I felt. My dad…well, he just looked beat-up.

One time (not my finest moment) when I was getting stronger, I woke to find my dad in the room. I had to look really hard at him. I think I was seeing a bit fuzzy. Having him there was a usual sight for me; only this time when I looked at him, he seemed far off somewhere. True, he was looking in my direction, but you could tell he was not seeing me. I will never forget the sorrow in his eyes. They glistened with tears that nearly fell to his cheeks. My father was looking at me as if I was already dead. My dad had that look. I was horrified! It was as if the weight of the world was on his shoulders. He was wrinkled, crumpled, and seemed so old.

How could he look at me that way? Didn't he see me? Dad, Dad, I'm right here! I'm not dead! I'm alive. I'm going to be fine. Can't you see that? He had tears in his eyes. One spilled over the rim. Again, such sadness. I was frantic! *STOP IT! Dad, please stop!* I mustered up everything I had, took a deep breath, and said in the most pitiful, raspy voice, "Dad, stop looking at me that way. I'm not dead! If you can't stop looking at me like I'm going to die, then you have to leave!"

He was jolted out of his trance. I had just slapped my dad in the face with my words. Without saying a word, he left quickly. He was devastated! His daughter, his Albondiga was dying. I looked like death. Of course he looked at me that way. He was helpless.

What did I do? Why would I have done that? What more pain could I have caused my father? I did that? With that one crude, drug-induced blow, I annihilated my father. How could I do that to my dear dad? I blamed the drugs.

The word got out. "Don't look at Letty that way, she gets very upset. We can't afford for her to get upset. If you can't fake it, don't go. If you feel yourself crumbling under the pressure, leave. Don't cry, don't do anything."

In the long run, the verbal ballistic missile did crush my dad, but it also worked. When you tell a sick person they look awful, it makes them feel even worse. You don't need words to convey this message either. The visitors would take a deep breath before they came in the room and looked as happy as they could, and they stayed just long enough for them to hold on. Later, I was told how they cried and held each other, wondering how long my body would hold on or how much more I could take. But it worked. I was feeling better. For the most part, the looks stopped but the glances to each other, those never stopped. Yeah, I saw those too. Sometimes I think people forgot I could see. Maybe they thought that all the tubes and wires obscured my vision.

My dad recovered from my verbal assault. I apologized, tears were shed, and we continued on the road to recovery.

12

Water of Life

I REALLY DON'T KNOW WHY I want to include a part about showers, except to say that sometimes people underestimate the power of this flowing gift. Spiritually, the symbol of living water gives us eternal life. As stated in a song by the Dameans, "Give us living water, we ask you, O Lord, that we never thirst again." Water is one of the elements of life that not only replenishes our body, but also refreshes our soul. It only makes sense that if one is deprived of this element, then one is depleted. I had not been allowed to bathe or wash my face and hair for a really long time. I was parched and drained!

My mom and the nurses had been giving me sponge baths, which were wonderful. My mom was the most loving and tender person to give me a sponge bath. Some of the nurses were pretty great too. It was a just a few nurses who really just wanted to be done with it. They weren't really gentle about my private parts and breasts. It seems that everyone had a really hard time cleaning my scar area. It was long, bloody, fragile, and gross. Some would tend to it; others just said it was too tender to touch. True, but all that encrusted blood made it harder to clean up when I finally could endure the clean-up pain. Some of the nurses wouldn't cover me up either they just wanted to be done with it. As I got better, I started to get embarrassed about my exposure. At first, I was too out of it to care. I'm sure I smelled of crusty old blood, surgery, and Betadine. Nice, and yet my loved ones still came to see me.

As the days passed and I started to get stronger, I needed a real shower! I had to find a way to submerge my entire body in water at the same time. I needed fresh-smelling soap, to be lathered up with great big bubbles, and foam rinsing everything off. I also needed my head washed! Dry shampoo in the seventies really didn't work very well. It just mushed your already vile hair around even worse. It was like spraying baby powder on my hair, making me look like a wet, matted, and mangy mutt. When I finally did get to the quickie shower stage, I was never alone and it was never for very long. Just a few minutes, almost like a camp shower—wet, lather, rinse, and you're done. I loved them anyway. I always finished feeling better than when I started.

Yes, I was dizzy. Yes, I was exhausted. But it didn't matter because I was getting cleaner and stronger each time I got in the shower. It was a very much like a great workout. I was always tired but happy. Water has always been my ally. But still, getting all that stuff off me would take months, and my hair…well, my hair would even take longer. Good thing I had a perm. Yeah, right!

13

Dreadlocks or Mop Top?

OH MY GOSH, IT'S HERE! The day they promised, the day I get to have my hair washed! In order for you to get the full picture of this gigantic event in my life, you really have to understand what I looked like. Here I am, a strong but weak person. I thought I was stronger because I was sitting, standing, rolling over, and begging for food. But what I didn't realize was just how bad I looked. Poor everyone who had to look at me. I have already explained the tubes and IVs, but just what did I look like?

Here is what I saw when I went to wash my hair. They were supposed to cover the mirror in the bathroom but they didn't. *Hoboy!* Prior to going to the hospital, I thought it was a good idea to get a curly perm, that way my hair would be easy to take care of (1970s remember?). Does a rat's nest conjure up any pictures? How about a rat's nest with dried blood? The surgery had taken over twelve hours so there was a lot of blood involved. The blood had to go somewhere, right? What had happened during the surgery was, the blood pooled down around the back of my neck. They sopped up most of it but a ton was left behind. I had clumps of dried blood literally stuck to my head. You could lift clumps of my hair from my scalp, it would be stiff and matted together. Man, did that ever hurt! It was really stuck on. My hair was so bad that dreadlocks would have been a blessing.

This is a Rastafarian hairstyle. Imagine the sound of steel drums playing reggae music with marijuana wafting through the air and Bob Marley singing "Get Up, Stand Up." Here I am revisiting my old drug style. But instead of a trench coat, I was now trading in the coat for a new druggie hairstyle. Dreadlocks involves washing, rolling, and twisting, never combing the hair until it appears as locks of rope. Getting any kind of brush or combing device through this type of hair is impossible. I was well on my way to my new do. Getting a brush or comb through my matted mess would take weeks...no, months. That was just the hair, then there was the bandage or gauze they used to cover the neck area. It felt like a California king-sized sheet covering my neck and half the side of my head. My face, lips, and eyes were swollen and droopy. Somehow my skin changed color from a nice dark brown to copper. My face, neck, and shoulders were Betadine-orange! I still had dried blood on the side of my face and all over my left ear. My teeth and tongue were in shades of gray. The surgical site was still too sensitive and not stabilized enough for the nurses to wipe clean. Cleaning me up from this rainbow mess was way down the priority line so they just left it there. Not too pretty. I still hadn't seen me yet. All I knew was that I wanted my hair washed. I knew I would feel better and stronger once I did that. It took a lot of convincing that I was strong enough but I really wasn't.

The team of nurses had to get multiple types of permission. I had to be wheeled into this huge shower then moved to a water-type wheelchair. They covered up my incision with different material so it wouldn't get wet. Since tissues and neck muscles were missing, my head seemed like a rag doll at times; other times it moved like a steel rod was jammed down my neck, creating a very big challenge for my nurses. Figuring out how to move my head either backward or forward was the biggest deal. My head didn't move much, sometimes flopping and freezing in place at other times. Not only did I look like the bride of Frankenstein, but I moved like her too! They finally figured it out. I had three nurses: one to hold me in the chair with the straps, another one to hold my head (I couldn't help because my left arm was still working like a wet noodle.), and a third nurse to wash me. They decided to lean me forward in the shower. The plan was set.

Trouble is, I was already exhausted before we started. When I was rolled into the shower room, I saw myself in the mirror and almost passed out. Who was that person looking at me in the mirror? It couldn't be me as I didn't recognize myself. I was the wrong color, fat-faced, and crusty! I started to cry (leakage), and I got faint. Ruckus! Scrambling!

"Take her back! No, let her stay!" Back and forth, they went. Should I go or should I stay? The nurses almost won (going back, that is). I knew they had gone to a lot of trouble to get me there. It had taken at least a couple of days just to set it up and many, many promises on my part and theirs.

I was dizzy and a bit nauseous but I had to pull it together. I was just about to break my first promise and barf all over their shoes! "Okay, okay, I am fine. Let's do this. I will feel better once it's over," I croaked.

They thought it was best if I stayed covered and then when it was over, they would put me in fresh hospital linens. This way, I wouldn't get chilled and waste my energy getting undressed and dressed again. One nurse was standing in front of me, gently grabbing my right shoulder and waist on the left side. She was straddling the giant water wheelchair. It looked like she was playing Twister, only standing and in the direct line of the water. She was going to get sopping wet. She leaned my body over and took the handheld shower nozzle, gently rinsing my head. The other two nurses were helping support my body so I didn't lean too far and fall. This is really a lot of work and a huge act of kindness and support on the nurse's part. They instructed me to close my eyes. I didn't realize why that was until I opened my eyes. Oops! Second promise broken. Do what they tell you.

Remember the scene in *Psycho* where the blood is running down the drain in the tub after she was stabbed? That was my scene, only there were gallons of blood swirling, swirling, swirling down the drain. My blood! *Oh my God, I'm bleeding to death! I pushed them too hard! I had to have my way, now I'm going to die from hair-washing!* I started to whimper.

They realized I had opened my eyes. Then they started to talk fast and explain. While they were explaining, they stopped rinsing. It had only been a few minutes but my body was giving out. I was passing out. Ruckus again! Man, I sure did cause a lot of that. Needless to say, they didn't get one tenth of the blood out. I didn't get my hair washed that day either. They used the smelling salts to bring me around. They toweled me off the best that they could and changed my soaking gown quickly.

I was awake, sort of. I was rolled back to the room. I tried to smile and act as if nothing had happened so we could do it again. My folks hadn't really been keen on the idea. I fooled no one. Not only was I a rinsed-off mess, but I was now a vampire-colored, rinsed-off mess. Every ounce of color had drained from my face. Great, now I looked and smelled like a wet, matted sheepdog that had just come in from the rain after playing in the mud all day! But I lived through it. I really had no chance of dying from this episode. I was back in my room, in bed and completely happy, although smelly and exhausted. I fell asleep before they could do anything with any of the messes. I didn't care, I was spent but felt great. Some of the blood on my face and ear was gone. I was refreshed and blessed with a new hairdo—dreadlocks. Rasta Mon!

14

Footprints

Footprints in the Sand
Mary Stevenson

One night I dreamed I was walking along the
    beach with the Lord.
Many scenes from my life flashed across the sky.
In each scene, I noticed footprints in the sand.
Sometimes there were two sets of footprints,
other times there was one set of footprints.
This bothered me because I noticed
that during the low periods of my life,
when I was suffering from
anguish, sorrow, or defeat,
I could see only one set of footprints.
So I said to the Lord,
"You promised me, Lord,
that if I followed you,
you would walk with me always.
But I have noticed that during the most trying
    periods of my life,
there have only been one set of footprints in the
    sand.
Why, when I needed you most, you have not
    been there for me?"

The Lord replied,
"The times when you have seen only one set of
 footprints in the sand
is when I carried you."

BY FAR, THE HARDEST PART for me was how I affected my loved ones. It's not about me but it is about me. I knew what was happening. I could see it in all of their faces. Was I going to make it? If I did make it, how would I end up? Would I talk? Teach? Be deformed? How long would I live? Did they get all the cancer? What would happen in the next surgery? The same questions would rise again for the second surgery. As I mentioned, we don't need words to say these things since our bodies speak volumes.

This part of the book may seem redundant. I repeat certain stories but it's from a different perspective. Things I thought I knew, I didn't, especially the part about coming out of surgery and being .01 percent alive. I got the percentage right, just the timing wrong. Why is all this important? It's back to that scribe person, your record-keeper. Years later, I had to unravel all this stuff. I just wasn't ready to go back to my past. Yes, I had been sharing the stories with many others, but to really go back, talk to everyone, and get new facts and stories, it just took me a long time. The most import aspect of this whole thing is that it was not meant to be told until now. Not all the variables were in place. I needed to live to this point so that I may tell this story from this perspective. If I had tried earlier, the facts would have been the same. I had cancer, I almost died, and I lost my voice. I used an experimental treatment, it worked. My faith, family, friends, music, and doctors pulled me through. But my perspective would have been very different. My voice would have had a different timber, rhythm, and resonance. It would have been the same song, only the arrangement would have been different. I don't think the fact that I got a few things wrong changes the outcome. Miracles are still miracles. I made it through with the grace of God.

I didn't have the answers to many of the questions yet I think I may have had a few answers without knowing it. As I got stronger,

I knew I was going to be all right. I didn't know how I knew, I just knew. Maybe it was after they told me that I would be able to make some sounds, perhaps even talk. Maybe it was after my first shower. I don't remember. I just felt okay, at peace. Many times, my mom would say that as I slept, I had an inner glow of radiance. No, they hadn't started radiation yet.

~My Mother's Footprints~

I've asked her many times after all these years how it was for her. She always said that she was sure God was going to take me home. She didn't want to leave the hospital for fear that when she returned I would be gone. The very first thing she did when she heard the doctor say cancer was run to the hospital chapel. She was praying and crying, crying and praying. When she finally would go home to rest, she would go to my bedroom, grab my pillow, and cry again, only to wake up and start all over again.

My mother was a very faith-filled woman. Piety, study, action, mass, and Eucharist were her life. She walked the talk. No mother is perfect. As with all families, there are times when you don't get along. We were no exception, we had our moments, but they were brief moments in our lives. I don't want you to get the wrong impression of my mom. Even though some of her friends called her Saint Bea, she was just my mom doing mom things.

Bea, as she was known, was a woman who didn't go unscathed from illness in her life. She grew up with a bad heart. Most of her life, she was ill and told that she might not live. She was told not to get married because it might kill her. She was told not to have children because it might kill her. She had three. Her tenacious will for living was passed down to me. Of course, we didn't know how much of this tenacity I had inherited until we both walked this path together. Just a bit of history about this great woman I call my mom, she suffered from three brain tumors, two heart attacks, and four stokes. She had also broken her back twice and suffered an assortment of others major medical illnesses. But talking to this 91-year-old wonder, you would never know she had endured that much. She thrived! She continued to teach us daily how to live life to the fullest. It is this gift that she gave and kept on giving to me. Our family had all learned that no matter what, offer your illness, pain, and suffering to God, remembering that there are always people worse off than you.

A mother's love is a force none can match. It is their life's blood that sustains you before you are born. A mother will give her very life for her child. There would be no moment of hesitation. There are millions of words expressing this love, books upon books. There is no sacrifice too large. My mom was no exception. She was at my bedside every day. She held my hand, wiped my brow, moistened my lips, and prayed with me. She prayed without me, counseled others, sat and watched me. She waited, waited, waited for that first moment when I would open my eyes. She waited for that first moment I could whisper "Mom," waited for the doctors to say they got all the cancer, and waited for me to move my left arm. She waited so much for me. She never gave up hope. She gave me so much strength and courage simply by waiting. My mom was there for all the triumphs. We all cried with joy when I could tilt my head back far enough to drink from a soda can for the first time. Every milestone, every tiny little step, she was there for me. How could I let her down? Now that's what you call FAITH (in capital letters).

Please don't get me wrong. Faith doesn't mean you stop crying. Faith doesn't mean you stop feeling pain for your loved one. It simply means that the grace of God is with you, that He is there holding you. This is the time you will only see one set of footprints in the sand. In fact, this was the time that poem became a source of strength for our family. My father embraced that story. Years later, we would print a copy of that poem for him when he was sick.

I truly believe that this was one of the many times God was carrying my family, especially Mother. I can picture God with my whole family being lugged on His back, leaving one set of profoundly deep footprints in the sand.

~Dad~

What a tremendous blessing it was to have had my dad. When I was little, I idolized him and followed him from room to room. As he walked down the block from work, he had a special whistle that would signal to Deb and me that he was almost home. When he would see us coming, he would take a knee, open his arms wide, and just wait for Deb and me to crash into him. I couldn't wait to see him. My life would have been different without Juan Rocha. I even look like him.

When I was two, one of my best memories was when I would pretend to be asleep so he would carry me from the car to my bed. He was strong, loving, and tender. He smelled so great too, an Old Spice woodsy smell. There was nothing my dad would not do for us. He would take us camping and fishing, made decks, repaired and painted fences, put things together, took things apart, and went on Sunday drives. He even showed us how to do the old soft shoe with sugar or salt on the floors to make the snazzy sound, just like in the old black-and-white flicks with Fred Astaire and Ginger Rodgers.

He was a top notch salesman. People loved him. They were drawn to him. He had charisma with a capital C. One of the best gifts he gave me was my ability to sell. He would say I was good enough to sell ice to an Eskimo or sell the skin off a rattlesnake while it was still alive. Now that was a confidence-builder. He did that too! He had a passion for life. He lived big and laughed bigger. You could hear my dad laughing from a block away. He had one of those wonderful contagious laughs that would make others join in or just smile with joy. Oh, could he ever spin a story! He was great at it, his friends couldn't wait to hear any Juan Rocha story. We all knew they were a bit exaggerated, but there was a kernel of truth to them. Besides, they were just fun to listen to.

Of course, he disciplined us. It was mostly my mother, but there was always "Wait until your father comes home." I was his Albonidga (meatball). Needless to say, I was a round, very chubby, roly-poly little baby. Thankfully, I grew out of that but never the nickname. Later on, he would shorten Albonidga to "Boingie." I had always been the number two daughter. I'm not sure why he liked to call us by numbers. John was never called number three. He would call Deb "daughter number one" and me "daughter number two." Being the second wasn't a bad thing, it just was my number order. My sister Deb was the first pride in his life—smart, funny, and quick witted, just like the old man. It just seemed like my dad never got over the fact that he and my mom had produced such wonderful kids. Whereas Deb inherited the "smarts," I got the art and music side, another pride for him.

He was thrilled when I picked up the guitar and asked him to teach me a few things. Artistic ability ran in the family. His brother studied at the Sorbonne in France and hung around Diego Rivera and Frieda Kahlo de Rivera. He was a professional artist, but I always thought my dad was better. No bias here.

Thank God for Deb. She kept the humor up in our time of need. Dad lost his; he was just sad. I believe it was unbearable for him. He was at a loss. Could he really lose his Albondiga? I remember seeing him lackluster and dull. He always looked hot even though hospitals are mostly kept on the cooler side. All throughout my time in the hospital, my dad always looked sweaty, uneasy, and out of place. He just didn't know what to do with himself.

Men are, by nature, fixers, but this was beyond him. He could not fix this; only God and the doctors could. It was out of his hands. Since my dad was a fixer, mender, seller, and action kind of guy, he was lost. He became so quiet. There was no loud laughter to be heard from blocks away, no jokes, no stories, no teasing. Nothing. He would just sit there and stare helplessly at me. If the tears got to him too badly, he would leave the room. This was still the era where men would not cry even if someone was dying. Many people from his store would come to see me in the hospital, reassuring him that the store was in good hands and all was well, which granted my dad the peace of mind to be present with his family and not at work. My dad showed all of his emotion on his face and body. Mom remembers him slumping and never really straightening up until years later. Since my dad really didn't talk about his feelings much, it was hard to get exact words. But body language can speak volumes. My dad had that look all over him.

Mom said for up to two years, dad was still waiting for the other shoe to drop. He was a religious man who had a strong faith in God. He gave his life over to God. However, this cancer was testing his faith too. He had such a hard time understanding why this had to happen.

His employees loved him. Dad's store was always a top seller. He taught his people how to sell and care for their customers. Simply put, honesty was the best policy in my dad's store. No, I think it was the only policy there. "Don't sell them something because you want the commission. Be honest. If it doesn't look good, tell them. Don't just sell it!"

He would emphasize that customers would be thankful and would always return, and they did. This is a technique that is true and noteworthy for selling and life. That's how my dad faced life—honest, straightforward, and respectful. Everything he did was led, first and foremost, by his faith. Therefore, when his employees saw my father devastated, this man that they would walk on the moon for, this man that never lacked in respect for them, they had to come. They only had to look at him to know how hard this was hitting him. My mother said even his suits looked rumpled. That is saying a lot. My dad was always a very crisp and spiffy dresser. He loved to wear and purchase clothes as well as sell them. It is a testimony to my dad's character that his workers came, not for me since they didn't really know me. They came for my dad to make him feel better. It was an act of love and respect for this man they called "Boss."

Deb recalls him being there, so sad and just sort of fading into the wall. At times, Deb says she can't remember seeing my dad, which is incredible because he was bigger than life to me. Nobody could ever miss my dad. Everyone knew when Juan Rocha was in the house, he commanded the room. For this man to fade into the wall is saying volumes on how it hit him. He lost weight, lost his tan, and lost his shine. Even his sales went down! Sometimes as he would sit in my hospital room, I would get mad because he would look at me *that way.* Other times, he would talk and I would listen; but mostly I received comfort from him just being there.

A few years later, he would make the most meaningful retreat in his life. It is called a Cursillo. During the weekend, a deeper relationship with Christ and a better understanding of the power of the Holy Spirit became a very profound experience for him. Long after I was healed, my cancer was still affecting my dad, leading him to go on this retreat and deepening his relationship with Christ. He realized that my survival was a message to people, an outward sign of showing the grace of God. He knew that I was a living, breathing miracle for all to see, a testimony in action. My time for putting this story on paper had not yet come. I wish he was here now so he could share with me his innermost thoughts and feelings.

As I improved, he started to come back to himself. I guess most people do that. Just remember, not everyone is on the same time clock. Some people need a bit more time to bounce back. I was staying with my folks after surgery. When he would get home, he would always ask how my day had gone. Mind you, I was in repair, not much was going on. But when I would tell him I ate soup or finally tilted my head back far enough to finish a can of soda, he would celebrate my little victory as if it was the most important thing in the world. That was my dad, always there. One thing my dad shared with me is that he always felt that God had given us a gift in my healing. He called it the gift of time. He would say we never know when God will take us home. He said that we each had a job to accomplish while on earth: to find the closest moments to Christ, be joyful, be thankful, show love, and remember to laugh so that we may live each day to the fullest. Juan Rocha was a very wise man. These were the standards he lived by.

~My Sister Deb~

One of the most interesting, brilliant, and hilarious people I know is my sister Deb. She works as a speech pathologist and has a true passion and calling for this job. Her skill has given her much notoriety among her colleagues in her field. The odd thing is some people either know only her smart side and others only her funny side. Her friends and family get to see both but mostly we see the funny side. This is important to the story because of all the people in the world, she could best describe to me what had happened to my voice so I could understand it better. She was also my scribe who was always ready to record notes to the doctors and questions we might have, a very important job and one Deb developed well because of her serious side.

Her recollection begins with her going with me on the second visit with Doctor Schafer. He had said that after doing the scan, there were two tumors, one at the base of the thyroid and one on the side of my neck. He felt that they were more than likely not related nor cancerous, but they would not know how extensive until they got into surgery. He also told my sister that the surgery would last about two or three hours. Deb says she didn't hear him say if "it did take longer, it would be cancer." What she does remember is that he said we should not worry. Dr. Schafer went into surgery not worrying and not expecting cancer. It should have been cut and dry. On surgery day after I got my IV and she passed out, I was wheeled out for the operation. The adventure began.

After many hours in the waiting room, Deb also recalled seeing the carts of food being delivered and the orderlies asking what room the surgery was in. Everyone knew it was for my surgery because they were the only ones left in the waiting room. Again, my folks asked if there was anyone they could talk to for information and again, nobody showed up to answer. Deb could hear the receptionist saying, "Yes, Mrs. Schafer. The doctor still is in surgery. No, I have no idea when he will be out but I will tell him as soon as he is finished."

The phone calls continued all night. Deb was well aware of what that meant. Her little sister was in trouble. The family was getting nervous. I think what really put them over the edge was when a new team of doctors went up to assist the current team. Deb watched as five new doctors showed up so Dr. Schafer and his team could rest a spell and eat. Still, no one came. Hovering over the receptionist put them in the right spot to see and hear a few things. They were trying to gain any kind of knowledge they could about me.

Now Deb had a bigger concern. It was not so much the surgery itself, but just how long could a body stay under anesthesia without causing brain damage? Finally, the doctor came out. I had cancer throughout my neck in a band of multiple tumors layered on top of each other. They had scraped the cancer off the vocal nerves, and the doctor wasn't sure if he had damaged or traumatized the cords. This is where Debbie really became pivotal. She immediately went from my sister to a skilled speech pathologist, comprehending the gravity of the situation then translating it into layman's terms for my parents. Deb later explained that he put the cords in an approximated position instead of letting them be wide open and frozen. If the cords had been left parallel to each other as they naturally are, I would have had zero chance of making any noise, let alone speaking. He placed them in a *V*-shape so I would have a breathy quality to my voice, providing the cords were not in shock or not permanently damaged. Allowing some air to get through would give me a strong whispery voice. But no one would really know until later.

It is at this point that listening and understanding becomes very difficult. It is always wise to have many pairs of ears. Later on, you can compare information and get a better understanding of what was said. Deb turned to the people in the waiting room, they heard it all. No matter where she looked, someone was crying somewhere. In the hallways and in the waiting rooms she could hear whispers of concern, questions of "will she make it", prayers, consolations and support. Deb hung in there.

She kept it all together for everyone until one day in my regular room after Joe got permission to bring in the album. I can remember the little cassette player sitting on the food tray. The music was beautiful. *Was that really us singing?* We were like angels. The harmonies were incredible. The tears began. *Keep it together.*

In walks Deb. Immediately, she sees, hears, and feels what is going on. Just as fast, her eyes fill with tears. The music is playing. She realizes that her baby sister helped to create this sound and she might never sing, let alone speak again or even live. This music playing may be the only means her family could hear my voice in the future. We connect, eyes to eyes, tears to tears. Then she left. It was too much for her. It broke her heart. All the holding in, all the emotions came flooding out in the hall. She had been the strong one up to that moment. Deb was the older sister and her job had always been the protector for John and me, but now as the music flooded her heart, it was just too much. Deb's life outside of the hospital, was already full of stressors. She remained calm, until she heard "that" song. It took her years—and I mean, years—for her to be able to be hear that song and not burst into tears. Now over thirty-five years later, she doesn't cry anymore. But when she does hear that song, bam! She is right there in the hospital, looking at her little sister lying on the bed with tears streaming while listening to the tape. It all comes back.

At the time, Deb and her husband Ralph had one child, Maricela. Their second daughter Renee, would follow a few years later. Ralph says he mostly remembers me being drugged and out of it. He is a man of few words, loving but quiet! He too was there the whole time, either at the hospital with Deb or watching Mari so Deb could be there. She never missed a day while I was in intensive care and the regular room but she finally returned to work after I had the second surgery. The doctor said I was on my way to recovery. I really don't know how she managed to get all that time off, but I do remember her always being there and giving me all her love and support, which really made a difference in my recovery.

Since Debbie is so funny, my mom was always taking her out into the hallway of the hospital and scolding her into brief moments of silence, insisting on no comedy routines. But things would always happen, and we would start to laugh again. Laughing really wasn't something I could do but the emotions were there. It would always end up in tears of laughter, pain or both. It didn't matter, we still did it. It was just Deb's way to help us all cope. Laughter is healing too, and all the tears of joy were worth it. It's funny but through all those memories, I can still remember laughing. There is nothing funny about dying and cancer, but somehow my sister could bring out the funny in anything.

One time when Deb came in to the hospital room, I was sitting out of the bed on a chair. As the nurse was giving me a sponge bath, she noticed long streams of tears rolling down my face and assumed I was having a hard time with movement and pain. I think what made it worse was that I couldn't talk much to express my pain level. Deb walked calmly over to me, cooing gently, "It's okay, Lett. You're going to be okay. We will get through this." She lovingly stroked my hand, a tender side I rarely saw from my sister. Not being able to talk audibly, I pointed pathetically down to my foot, tears continuing to fall. She looked and saw the heavy nurse standing right on my foot with her full weight, grinding down each time she moved. I guess she thought she was standing on the folds of sheet that covered me. I tried to tell her in my feeble way but she must have thought I was getting upset because they had maneuvered me into a chair and I was in pain. She continued to bathe me, saying, "It's okay, honey. It's okay."

Please note that I'm crying about foot pain. Now that is real progress! Whenever I got out of bed, my legs would fall asleep, which made standing very difficult. I was weak and would start to tremble. Additionally, I still had tons of tubes sticking out of me so manipulating all this stuff was a big challenge and an ordeal.

When Deb finally got her off my foot, she finished quietly and then left. We started laughing. As Deb said we got a lot of "material" off of that one incident. There were many more incidents of that kind. That's how Deb is. The glass is not just half full but overflowing for her. She can always see the funny side of anything. I love her very much. She was and is a blessing to many.

~Joe~

When Joe was out of high school looking for a mass to play at, he joined my nine thirty group. He was the same age as my brother and pretty easygoing. We hit it off right away. He sang with us for about a year. When I graduated from college and left for South America, I put him in charge of the singing group saying, "Take good care of my group, I'll be right back!"

But when I returned home briefly for my brother's wedding, my group had changed so much. It was now Joe's group, and they were thinking about cutting an album. Joe had been sending me all the new music they had been learning. Since there wasn't much to do in

Barranquilla during the week, I practiced every day so I became really good at it. At times, the music was the only thing that made me feel normal. I actually had cancer then but didn't know it yet. I was feeling off and very lonely so learning the music and playing my guitar gave me many hours of comfort, which kept me going. In June when I got home from South America, we cut the album right away. I was in the hospital by July and doing music ministry with the group by September. There you have it, cut and dry!

We called ourselves the Sounds of the Son, and we were really pretty good. We did all the latest Catholic cover songs. We did concerts around San Diego County, a few in Los Angeles, as well as seminars and workshops. We were in demand. We were going to be famous! Our music was very powerful, and it became an integral part in my recovery. It fed my heart and soul. We touched so many, sometimes even making people cry. Joe and I had a lot in common and became great friends. He was fun, talented, dedicated to his music, and loved to sing. When Joe heard that I was ill, he became a force that lived in the hospital. It seemed every time I woke up, the guy was there.

On the day of surgery, Joe showed up later in the afternoon, thinking he could just check on me and be on his way. Everyone had the same idea of popping in and out. But when he arrived around four, he was shocked to find that I was still in surgery and no one knew anything. He decided he was not going to budge until he had seen me despite falling asleep a few times and ignoring my mother's encouragement to go home. He just stayed. No, Joe was not going anywhere. He needed to stay, he wanted to stay; and he had to stay. I don't remember if Joe was working at that time. I can't imagine him not having a job. Everybody worked and went to school. That's how it was done back then—school, work, boyfriend, or girlfriend. That was the norm. But for Joe to be there at the hospital every day, he either wasn't working or he had lost his job because he was with me. All I knew was that Joe was always there.

Poor Joe was either dozing, going to get food for the family, or in deep conversation with my sister Deb. He understood they didn't want to leave the area in case the doctor came out so that left it up to him. He was the gofer and did his job well.

He and my mom became very close while I was in Columbia. He remembers their long daily visits swimming in the pool and my mom making him lunch. He thought he was keeping my mom company while I was gone. I think it was the other way around. He missed me a lot while I was away, and the time he spent with my mom was very special to him. Now it only seemed right that he would support his new family. Joe put in the long hours, showing his loyalties. He not only stayed, but came every day, never missing a day. He never left my side or my parents' side. He was their personal servant, always at the ready. Debbie can't remember not seeing Joe there. No one questioned him, assuming he was just family. The doctors and nurses were used to him already so he easily gained access to intensive care.

Joe was so relieved to see me on the gurney even if I did look dead. He cried as he saw me, proclaiming and laughing to everyone that I had winked at him. Now I realize that Joe might have been a little bit in love with me. I'm not sure if it was romantic, my aunt Grace thought so. For me, it wasn't. For Joe…well, it's something we never talked about but it was love. Since there are so many forms of love, I will leave it at that. As Joe recalls, it was a whirlwind. As it turned out, he was working and going to the hospital every day. He was exhausted. He told me he lost ten pounds while I was in the hospital. Go figure! I think I found his ten pounds, and I wasn't even eating. Men!

All the time I was in the ICU, the group was waiting for the album to come out. Making a real live record was a big deal, but it took time to press the records, make the jacket, and box them. Finally, the record was done, and Joe couldn't wait for me to hear it. I was kind of busy at the time, and the doctors and nurses kept delaying him. Joe was way cool because he had a portable cassette player. Wow, mobile music! You didn't even have to lug around a record player! I know these things had been out for a while but just as in everything, the cost was dropping drastically so nearly everyone could afford to get some sort of mobile recording device eventually.

My dad even bought me a small cassette player so I could hear ABBA while I was recovery.

After Joe got permission, he set the player on the little rolling food table in my room. As per the rules, he was ready to stop if I got too excited. The doctor had been very clear on that point. Hospital rules are less strict now so what Joe was to doing was big. It hadn't really been done before. It does sound rather strange that someone bringing in a cassette player could cause such a ruckus in the hospital, but hey, everything has to be new once! The whole floor was talking about this guy who was bringing in a sound system (cassette player) of an album that they had recorded. We became the celebrities of the hospital, we were famous. I slept away my fifteen minutes of fame! Word has it that Joe even sold a few albums that day! He was so excited and told me to relax and close my eyes. He had already cued up the first song he wanted me to hear. It started. "Before the sun burns bright..." *Oh my gosh, that was us!* I could hear all of our voices. Wow, it was incredible! I couldn't believe we sounded that good. *Us! Was that really us singing?* We were like angels. The harmonies were so smooth. We blended as one.

We were just regular people who sang at Sunday mass. Our friendship had brought us to this moment, and Joe and I were finally listening to the long-awaited album. It suddenly hit me. *Would I ever get to sing again? Play the guitar? Make this beautiful sound with my friends?* Oh, I so wanted to. It was like a new drug as it began to course through my veins. I wanted more; I needed more. I had to sing and play forever! It was as if he could read my mind as Joe's eyes filled with tears. He knew what I was thinking and feeling right at that very moment. I had tears leaking down my face but I couldn't let the nurses see how upset I was becoming. I had to keep my emotions in check because I knew the rules. I had to stay in control. I couldn't allow the music to stop. I now needed that music to feed my soul to help me get through the unknown.

The air in my room seemed heavy, dense, and felt just as if a tornado was going to touch down. I could almost see the angry clouds swirling above me just before the cone of destruction touched down on the earth. How would I make it through this? How would this end? Joe and I locked eyes. He knew. Joe could see and feel my anguish.

Just then, Deb entered right into the thick of it, and she made all the unspoken connections. It is too much for her to bear. Her emotions are raw. She starts to cry then quickly leaves the room. Joe sees it all happen. He calmly lets the song end, explaining that I should rest a bit. He does this rather quickly so he could catch up to Deb. He instantly sees that she is in need and goes after her, leaving the cassette player there so I could listen to it. I fall asleep with the music. As he catches up to Deb, no words were spoken. They hugged a long, knowing hug. There were still many questions yet to be answered.

Joe remained faithful to my family. He was at the hospital every day and at my house as I recovered. We continued our friendship, sharing in my recovery and our love of music. These moments and more are part of our history. Nothing will ever change that. As we continued to grow up, our lives slipped apart. Many years later, we were to be reunited again at St. Pius. Only then, he was my boss, a Catholic priest. Father Joe Masar remained true to my mom, coming to her in her many times of need. I am forever grateful to him for that. We would never rekindle our deep friendship although we do see each other occasionally. Our past is still filled with so many wonderful (some sad) memories of faith, music, cancer, and our deep friendship.

~Little Brother John~

Ah, my little brother. My guy, my palsy-walsy, as we used to call each other. Now for some reason, it's bro and sis. We have always been close. In our youth before he got married, John and I did everything together. He was my best friend. But as life goes on, new friends are made, new paths are taken, and new adventures begin with others. John was blessed when he found Terri, his loving wife. They have been married for over thirty-five years, have four wonderful children, and still live in Colorado.

John remembers me going to the doctor before his wedding in April. The doctor wanted me to stay and do more tests to figure out what the lump was. John always wondered why I disregarded the doctor's advice of staying. All he knew was that I returned to Colombia to finish my first year of teaching and go see the world.

Now that school was out, they would leave on their delayed honeymoon after being reassured that my surgery was supposed to be routine in and out with some recovery at home. John figured if nobody else was worried, then he wouldn't be either. It seemed clear-cut so they left for their Colorado camping honeymoon in July. They fell in love with the Rocky Mountains and decided this is where they wanted to begin their life and raise their family; that is, just as soon as John finished his schooling. He also promised he would stay in contact via telephone booth. They were having a wonderful time, sometimes even forgetting to call. They just arrived at Telluride, stopped for late lunch, and called from the restaurant. When they heard that the surgery had taken twelve hours, they were in shock. I had cancer, they had not gotten it all, and I would need a second surgery. I was in intensive care and fighting for my life. My blood pressure was extremely low, and I was not breathing on my own. It looked bad.

Everyone wanted John in San Diego now! It was already late afternoon, when they arrived at camp. Still in shock, they just didn't know what to do, so they set up camp and went for a long walk to make plans. They both decided it was just too late to start back and besides, they had been driving all day, and were exhausted. On their walk they found themselves sitting at the edge of the world on a flat rock, watching the sunset overlooking the valley. It would have been perfect, it was beautiful, and one of those scenes you see on a calendar, breathtaking. But they were hundreds of miles away. How did this happen? It was then that it hit John, he might lose his sister. They were so far away, how could they ever make it in time? Even if they drove all night, I might be dead when they got there. From the sounds of the report it seemed as if they would be going home to my funeral.

Had he said goodbye to me? What were his last words to his sis? He was in torment. What was going to happen? He stood up on the rock next to Terri and began to cry. Then in anger, he yelled, "Why, God, why? Why have you done this to my sister? She never did anything. She doesn't deserve this. It's not fair!"

After tears and long moments of silence, they returned heartbroken to their campsite. That night, they talked in hushed tones over the campfire. It was decided. They would cut their honeymoon short and drive straight through to San Diego. Despite their exhaustion, they began to pack up. Terri would stop to comfort John as he cried, realizing that their 4:00 a.m. departure was coming soon. It was the longest drive home. They stopped looking at the beautiful scenery and drove in silence on pins and needles. When they did stop, John tried to get to a phone booth but they were in the mountains and sometimes the calls wouldn't go through even if they could find a pay phone. Time was ticking by, and they had no control. What would they find upon their arrival?

He remembers finally getting to the hospital and running to see me. I was asleep. He also thought I looked okay, kind of peaceful. That part does ring true. Many people said that I had this special look about me. It makes me happy to know that John saw it too even though he had missed all the exciting parts. He went to search for my dad. My mother understood that this was something John had to do with my father. They left together for what seemed like hours. John remembers Dad crying and being afraid. It was impossible for either John or Terri to comprehend all that my family had gone through these past days, but at least they were there now. While John was with my dad, Terri was with my mom and sister, trying to get the facts straight. They were relieved to find me on the mend, out of immediate danger, and not dead.

After the second surgery, John remembers going in and out of my hospital room and seeing my improvement. He felt relieved. Everyone was excited when the doctor said I would be able to talk somewhat and that it appeared as if they had gotten all of the cancer. The surgery was considered groundbreaking and was a true success. As for me, I mostly slept. I can't remember John being there at all.

These memories—or rather lack of memories—are very hard for me. I wanted him there with me the whole time. Then when he got there, I can't remember him! I feel so badly about that. I don't know why I can't remember him. It's funny because I can remember so many other silly details, but my beloved brother, my palsy-walsy, nothing. It took me years to admit this to him, and I felt better knowing that he too had a very blurry impression of that time. Even after all these years when we talk about this, it's still fuzzy.

I know my brother was there. I know he prayed with my family, giving love and support, and being given love and support in return. That's the most important part of my brother's side of the story. He made it back in time. I didn't die, and he was able to be there for my dad. How long after the second surgery did he stay? I don't know. Well, it really doesn't matter. He did what he could do.

~Mary~

There are so many feelings, so many mixed emotions of so long ago. Still, I think one of the most painful memories was with my friend Mary. The dreadful day began well after all of the surgeries. I had begun driving, mostly so I could go to daily physical therapy and not continue to burden my parents. I had just been to physical therapy and then drove over to Mary's house. This became my new routine because I really couldn't do much yet. It was sort of a field trip for me to drive twelve miles from Chula Vista to San Diego. I was eating and drinking like a regular person, sometimes we would even go out to eat. I was definitely recovering well and getting stronger every day.

There I was standing in her cute little rented house, leaning on the door jamb in the kitchen, and she was washing dishes. It was early evening. Some memories still remain as if they happened yesterday. I was excited because that day, we had done the spider walk with my fingers climbing up the wall. I got my left arm up further than it had been in months. I still had little control so when it got to a certain level, my arm would come crashing down with a thud. Still, it was exciting for me to see it moving up the wall. The crashing part would get fixed later.

Mary was listening to me talk about what I had done and accomplished that day. She then turned to me and began to yell, "Is that all you have to talk about? Physical therapy? Isn't there anything else you have to say? It seems that all we ever talk about is you and your cancer!" She was really angry.

Why? Bam! I had just been slapped. *What just happened? Is that really all I talked about? Was it really always about me and my cancer? Besides, I was talking about physical therapy, not cancer.* I really had no life other than that. I was almost ready to go back to work, true, but I didn't have a job and I was still living at home. But, hey, I had started to pretend to sing and play my guitar. I was driving and doing other stuff too. *Why was she yelling at me? What did I do?*

Then she told me how she didn't see us having anything in common anymore and that maybe we should take a break from being friends! In addition, the rest of the group all felt the same. They really didn't want to hang out with me anymore! *Wait, what? What did I do? What did I just say? Where was this all coming from?*

Devastated and speechless (again, not so funny because now I was talking), I didn't know what to say as my eyes filled then overflowed with tears. My throat began to constrict, and I became light-headed. This I could not understand. I could, and would survive the cancer, but losing my core group and my best friend, how was I going to deal with that? This was my friend Mary who went to Los Angeles with my sister and folks to pick me up when I returned from South America. She wrote all the time while I was gone and even sent me cassettes so I could hear all my friends' voices. She would carry around the cassette player, filling sixty or even one hundred and twenty minutes of daily stuff for me to hear. Okay, some of the stuff might have been a bit boring but it was the thought that counted. It made me feel connected to them, and I really felt like I knew all the things they were doing. I would receive a tape from her each month. I felt included. We were the best of friends. Mary came nearly every day to the hospital and visited regularly at my folk's house. *What was happening? Does she really mean this?* She was the leader of our little group, the organizer, and the planner.

I had been friends with some of these girls in high school, then we added college friends, and a couple of the girls were friends of friends. We just clicked and became a tight group. Prior to me leaving for South America, we used to go every weekend dancing and clubbing. It was our life, all of us. Nobody got really drunk or anything, but we would have our stomping grounds and we were the faces in many of the nightclubs in Mission Valley. I would get home at two or three in the morning, get up, and then go to sing at church on Sunday. We would start with happy hour on Thursday and then dance the weekends away. I did this throughout college with the same group of girls.

What did they mean they didn't want to hang out with me? Nothing in common? True, I wasn't clubbing with them. I was still kind of weak, and a lot of activities would just wear me out. *So dancing and clubbing? Hmmm, not yet. Plus, who would want to dance with a scarred-up girl?* I did go to their apartments for dinner. We hung out, we laughed, and we told stories. *Boring? I was boring?* Not wanting to create more of a scene, I turned as tears continued falling from my eyes. I left without a word, never to return. *What had just happened?* I cried all the way home. Now I was depressed. To think that I endured this whole process and coped okay with it, only to be devastated by my friend. *Wow, I was losing friends because I didn't die. Incredible!* It was shortly after that when I started to seek professional help.

This is where age plays an important part in this story. It would take me over twenty-five years to find out why that had really happened. Here is what Mary told me. It seems that my dear friend had more than one person in her life with cancer. Both of us were dying. One did die. On top of that, her dad was going through some extremely hard times, and he would later take his own life. To make matters worse, Mary was in her car one day when a wasp flew in an open window and stung her repeatedly. It was so awful that she had to go to the hospital. All she could think about was getting out of the hospital. To her, bad things happened in a hospital. She didn't want to "catch" cancer. All she knew was that her two closest friends both had cancer and had been in a hospital. Now she too was in a hospital. It was just more than she could bear. She was afraid that cancer was going to get her next. As irrational as it may seem, this is where Mary was. Fear gripped her.

Then there was the final nail in the coffin of my doomed friendship. Mary thought, *What do I do with you now?* She had been ready for me to die, but I didn't! She said, "You just weren't the same person anymore. You were quieter, weaker, and not as much fun. You couldn't laugh much and when you did let go, you had a coughing fit, which then reminded me that you are still sick and might die!" Mary explained that I got tired all the time. I was always clearing my throat and speaking with a raspy voice. "Plus," she continued, "we can only do one thing at a time, like either dinner or a movie, never both. Forget about going dancing and clubbing! Would you ever recover and be the same?"

She wanted the old Letty back. To Mary, it seemed impossible. She already lost one friend, she didn't know what was wrong with her dad. Now she had lost me even though I didn't die. Remember, cancer was cancer and few lived, which meant I probably was going to die anyway. The absolute final crushing blow was that she couldn't watch another friend die from cancer! Mary was going through a lot for a twenty-five-year-old. There were so many unanswered questions about her father. The wasp incident finished it for her. I mean, really, how many coping skills do we have when we are twenty-five? The best way for her to deal with it was to remove the reminder—me! It was the only thing she could control. The others mostly went along with it. "Where's Letty? Umm, she's at home." Soon, they all just stopped asking, coming around, or calling.

It took me years to get over that one and some maturity to realize that my old friends could only do so much. I still don't blame them. We have discussed it and made amends. It's all good now, but it was a valuable lesson, nonetheless. As I think back on the day in the kitchen, it may have helped me deal with the situation had I known the reasons for her reaction, anger, and frustration. I may not have known the reason for my cancer, but if I had known everything Mary was going through maybe, just maybe, it would have played out differently. Something I will never know.

~Tom~

Before I left for South America, my boyfriend at the time promised to write while I was gone. But he didn't. Not once, not even a postcard! When I returned home, not yet having gone to the hospital, we met. I was just so hurt, mad, crushed, and brokenhearted. Tom really meant a lot to me. I thought we were going to have a future together. Marriage? We didn't know. It was serious but not so serious that I didn't leave for South America. Poor guy never knew what hit him. Now I know it was my lack of hormones.

My mother remembers Tom coming over and him having zero idea of what was just about to happen. He sat in the tall, padded rocker in the living room. It started out okay but it soon escalated. All my emotions got the best of me. I began to raise my voice and yell, "If you couldn't take the time to keep in touch with me while I was thousands of miles away, then I must not be that important to you." I would have screamed even louder because I was so upset, but screaming was a thing we never did in our home. Well, neither was yelling, but I'm going to blame it on the lack of hormones. He tried to explain but nothing he said rang true. Mom also told me that when she heard me crying, she just crept off to the back bedroom and closed the door. We broke it off. I was worse off. Wow, I thought, I guess I was more in love with Tommy than I realized. Whatever the reason, his tremendous lack of communication just fell flat. He could have used a tape recorder like Mary!

We both graduated from San Diego State that year. I went off to teach. He wasn't sure what he was going to do so he took up selling "masterpieces" in a truck that went across the United States. "Why have prints when you can own your very own oil masterpiece? For one day only, go to the "blank" hotel and select your very own oil painting. Prices vary, selection is limited. Hurry, hurry, before you lose this wonderful opportunity!" Tommy was the guy who would drive the truck from city to city, setting up shows, hiring help, and then moving on. He was sort of a modern-day gypsy. He did this the entire year I was in Barranquilla. When he heard from his parents that I was in the hospital and in very grave condition, he came rushing back. He drove nonstop from back east straight through to Chula Vista.

Wow, two guys in love with me at the same time, and I didn't even know it! I know, but thank goodness this book is not called, *Let's Analyze Letty's Love Life*! Both guys handled my cancer in two completely different ways. When Tom finally came to see me in the hospital, he was scared. Yes, scared of me for my anger, my hurt, and my confusion as to why he never wrote. It was as if he had fallen off the planet. He promised to remain in contact. We were boyfriend and girlfriend. We had been together (not biblically) on the last night before I left, whispering of a future together. Were we really going to be together? I mean, really, really, together like marriage when I came back? Would that have been my future if I hadn't gotten cancer? I will never know.

He wondered just how upset I would be. Would I lash out at him again, screaming and yelling? Well, maybe yell, but not scream. Tom didn't realize there was no way I could do either since I could barely speak. Would I even want to see him? Would I kick him out of my hospital room? How badly off was I? His mom said I had been in great danger of dying but I was now much better, awaiting my second surgery. I was accepting visitors for short stays. He remembers me crying, doubting my decision to go to South America. He encouraged me, saying we were young and it was the perfect time to have this adventure. He was convinced I would regret not going. Did he advise me correctly?

He missed me so much he had to see me. He might even get fired but he just sort of rushed through the last job to get back quickly. By the time Tom got back, so much had already happened. I was now sitting up in my bed in a regular room, a huge step in my progress. I almost had all of the tubes pulled out, except the IV, and I was also whispering a bit. My hair was still a bloody matted mess, my color was a deathly gray-brown, and my teeth looked like they would fall out of my mouth at any time. Mostly all visits were pretty short and pretty quiet.

When Tom showed up, he actually brought a friend! He was a really cute guy who had brown hair, and a very kind smile. But wait,

I'm dying. Well, not dead yet as I was checking this guy out! *Was I really checking this guy out? Yes, I was!* Tom looked shocked, his jaw dropped. He was unable to talk. He just wasn't expecting to see what he saw. Hey, I looked great in comparison to my prior deathly pallor. No one had a chance to prepare him. I saw it in his face.

Horror! I looked horrible! What was Tom thinking? How could he bring this really cute guy in my room to meet me when I am dying? Considering they couldn't hear me through the bandages, grossness, coughing, and falling asleep, I think I was as nice as a dying person can be. Great first impression, don't you think?

When Tom introduced his friend, he had to clear his throat a few times. We chatted a bit and then they quickly left. I never did date the cute guy but it did cross my mind. I looked dreadful! I was even more furious with Tom. Why would he do such a thing? It turned out, Tommy was using his friend as a human shield in case there was a second nuclear blast from me. He was hoping that by bringing his friend, I would be too polite to say anything about his absence in my life for the past year. Man, was that the wrong choice! He had just made it a million times worse! His fear drove him to bring a complete stranger to meet his ex-girlfriend on her death bed. *Oh, Tommy!*

As for Tom not writing, the guy was dyslexic and never wanted me to know. He was too embarrassed to have me find out. He got through college only with the help of his family. It was their secret. He was afraid I wouldn't love him if I knew that he couldn't write. See, back then, we didn't know about dyslexia. We just thought someone was really dumb when they couldn't write or spell. But I'm dyslexic too and, thankfully, I did understand. When he finally did explain why he hadn't written, it all made sense and rang true. For that reason, we resolved our problems and remained great friends for many years.

But I had changed, not just from the cancer but also from my trip abroad. We were no longer the same people. He changed too. Being on the road alone for a year gives a person a lot of time to think. Years later, my Tommy would die in an ultralight plane crash, and I will forever miss him.

~The Others~

This is a section of my Willow family, my singing group, the Sounds of the Son, and an event with my aunts. They remain important because it's part of my development either before, after, or during the cancer.

I begin with my aunts' story because it was an awakening for me. As rotten as this may sound, I used my illness to my advantage. As in all families, there are disagreements. It seems that both of my aunts were having one of those times for about three years. Most of my visits were pretty nice because the visitors had all been warned about the look. There was lots of chitchat, mostly on their part, but I had gained a bit of my voice back and would add a few tidbits when I could. Since one of my aunts was sitting right in front of me, I thought *Aha, opportunity!* I knew I was "bad off," but, hey, my statistics were getting better every day so I went for it. I would use what God gave me. You know, sort of take the bull by its horns. My two aunts had been quarreling for a long time. I again mustered up my strength. Hadn't I learned anything from my comments to my dad? I said, "You and your sister have been fighting for a long time. It's time to make up. You never know when you are going to die. You might never have the chance to fix things." She started to cry. She said I was right and she would talk to her.

Hey, it worked! What else can I fix? That was it! My mom put a stop to me right then and there. "No more fixing family problems!" *But wait, I'm good at this.*

It was then I first realized that having cancer made people listen to me. I really didn't get it that much, just that people stopped talking because they wanted to hear what I had to say. Never mind that my voice was just a croaky whisper or that they got tired of saying "What?" I guess cancer doesn't affect self-confidence. Man, I really was full of myself!

~The Sounds of the Son~

We were not just a singing group, we were a family. We laughed until we nearly peed our pants, cried until we ran out of Kleenex, and fought so loud and hard that we would either start to cry or laugh at the absurdity of it all, just like we were brothers and sisters. Part of our dynamic was because we had four people from one family. Pops Leonard, the sixty-year old dad, and his three kids (ages twenty-three to forty): Donna the oldest, Tom right after, and Kathy just a bit younger than me. In addition, our group also had Lorraine, Mike, Pat, and Laura (the youngest at sixteen), and myself, plus, Joe, of course, our fearless leader. He, along with San Diego's own Father Joe Carroll, got us so many gigs. The more we sang, the better we got and the more places we would go to perform. The Leonard's voices already blended beautifully because of their DNA and from years of singing together. The rest of us just meshed with them. With Joe's guidance, we created a one-voice sound that you couldn't hear any one specific voice. It became our eleventh voice. How we found each other was another gift from God.

When we were in our prime and things were right with us, it was wonderful. The Holy Spirit not only touched the hearts of the people we were singing to, but ourselves as well. Sometimes we were even moved to tears. We would even tease Tom Jr. about drifting off to another planet, sort of "jelling out" as he sang. I later understood and experienced that he was being so affected, transfixed by the Holy Spirit that he was lost in that moment of tonality, rhythm, sacred words, and spirituality.

When I think back on the Damean's songs "The Lord Is Near" or "You Are My Sons", the words are so touching. The notes were so perfectly combined that it seemed hard to improve them. But our harmonies were new, even to the original artists. This was our gift, our blending the soothing sounds that was created by our voices. That's what did it. It was this combination of voices that caressed me and made me want to make more music, to crave the feeling of being closer to God than ever before. That is the most incredible feeling in the world. It's how it made me feel and how it made others feel. That's the gift. God's plan was never for us to make it rich and famous, it was to learn to pray through music with and for people.

My singing and guitar playing had become the most fulfilling way for me to praise God. It was something that I lost and regained through hard work and perseverance. This is my deepest form of prayer. People have told me that they can sense God's presence through our music. As my heart beats rapidly and I release the last breath of air from the song, I am overcome. I can't believe I am still doing this. It's perfect.

~Willow School~

As I reflect back, music was part of the passion and purpose, but the other major love in my life was teaching. I fell in love with that as a child. I had always gone to Catholic school as a child and just knew I wanted to be a teacher. I also thought I wanted to be a nun because the only way you could teach was to be a nun, right? Wrong. When I found out I could teach without being a nun, my career was set, so were my goals. I think I wavered for five minutes in wanting to be an architect. In the seventies, career choices were just beginning to change for women. Although women nurses, teachers, and home-makers were still the norm, there were now lady doctors, lawyers, and architects who were beginning to stretch the boundaries. It really didn't matter to me what new frontier was developing for women, I just wanted to teach.

Whereas God was my spiritual haven, Willow School was my earthbound harbor. It gave me a purpose, a meaning, and the will to persevere through all obstacles. Through the guidance of John Gurgerty, the assistant principal, I weathered the storm for the next few months. I believed teaching was what I was supposed to do. I had been substituting throughout the San Ysidro School District and settled on two school sites. I really liked both of the principals very much but there was just something about Willow, the staff, and parents who seemed friendlier and more open.

John had asked me to take a seventy-two-day contract in March. I had to let John know that I might not make it to the end of the year.

My prognosis was still not that great, the jury was still out. Life was not a guarantee. I was still weak and tired most days but by March, I was feeling better and stronger. When I told him that I might be dead before the year ended, his response was, "We will cross that bridge when we get to it." Later, I realized that I had worked so hard because he had entrusted me with my own classroom. He could have given that job to any number of substitutes but he gave it to me, a young teacher with just one year of teaching under her belt, who may die at any time, who's voice faded away before the end of the school day, and who was still going to physical therapy because her left arm was not working properly. Still, he trusted me.

How could I die on him? I used to call him my hero because he just made me believe that everything was going to be all right. He just knew it so I just knew it. John was awesome. He put so much trust in me and made me feel that I could do anything. He took me under his wing as well as my new Willow family. There was my purpose!

What brought our staff together and made us so unique is how we all supported one another. There was a true love there. We really cared for each other. Our lunchtime was a very special time for us. We all sat together, talking about our concerns, families, pets, kids, you name it. We were all involved. Yes, just like a real family, there were arguments. You are closer to one brother or sister but if anyone of our staff members was in true need, we would be there for that person. It was that spirit of service, love, concern, and support that I felt when I first got there.

I have to say that my first class was really tough. I had a core group of little gems I thought of as my "Samurai 7." I had a sociopath who couldn't or wouldn't be diagnosed because then he would be labeled for life. I also had an exhibitionist (Yes, he would drop his trousers and underwear whenever he had an audience.). I had two bullies and three "extremely naughty" kiddos, one of whom actually knocked me over with a crashing blow to the area where my cancer still might be! At times, I felt like I was playing ping-pong, bouncing from one problem to the next. My first year of teaching really didn't help me much with those kinds of problems. All I had experienced in Barranquilla was a bunch of overly entitled, really sweet rich kids who never got in fights in the classroom and then hit the teacher.

My voice was still very weak and I was exhausted from the cancer, getting my thyroid meds in order, as well as physical therapy. I would hold it together just long enough for them to leave for the day then I would cry, go home, and crash. I would get up, teach, go to therapy, come home, eat something, and then go to bed until the next day. I would repeat the same cycle until Friday. I would sleep most of Saturday, go to church on Sunday, then back to bed until Monday morning. It was excruciating. I did finish that year only through the grace of God and that Willow spirit. In retrospect, I don't think I would have made it if I didn't have my guardian angels holding me up on both sides and my new Willow family supporting my back and front.

Sometimes, what is remembered is how people can shine in the darkness when faced with the suffering of others rather than the words they have spoken. Over thirty years later, Willow has always remained the constant I needed throughout my years of teaching. I don't think I would have made it without that wonderful core of friends.

Part 2

The Middle

15

Phase Two of Two

THE NEXT STEP, SURGERY NUMBER two. In comparison, this surgery was really easy—well, at least the physical part. All they had to do was open up the right side of my neck and take out the rest of the cancer. The problem was that I surprised them last time. What they thought would be a two- or three-hour procedure turned into an incomplete marathon. To say that everyone was apprehensive was putting it mildly. I had tons of people pray over me. I saw a bazillion (again, not a medical term) doctors prior to the surgery. I knew the best-case scenario but not the worst case. They didn't want to tell me.

Why not? Would I talk again or would I become permanently mute? Was the right side of my neck going to look all mangled like my left side did now? Hey, a new question, would I be able to hold my head up by myself if they took more muscle tissue? Would I have to wear a neck brace all the time? Was I going to die? How long did I have? What about my right arm? Would it become a vegetable? Would the surgery take as long? Was I going to get back on morphine and was I going to be back in intensive care? Why did I have so many questions? Hadn't they prepared me for this?

The nurses answered most of the questions, but I guess it didn't satisfy me. Did I sound a bit panicky? I think so. My drug-induced brain never stopped questioning as I was soon to be rolled down the hall into a tsunami of unknowns. It started the same as before, becoming very busy with prayers, kisses, hugs, and drugs, except for a sister who didn't pass out. Mom said morning mass was offered for me. A bunch a people were already saying rosaries. There were tears, more kisses, and more hugs. Hugs were difficult. Everything still hurt, and I was hooked up like a Christmas tree in July. More kisses. *Didn't you guys already do that? I feel like you are sending me off to war never expecting me to return.* I held back tears of apprehension. Down the hall I went, toward my new future. How would I return?

The black-and-white reels are running, the sound of film is cracking. Cue music, "The cruel war is raging." My parents are holding hands, watching helplessly. They bend down one last time to kiss me. Just like war when you send a loved one away and you never really know the outcome, I seem to be at that juncture. I am going in for the next battle. It was clear they feared they would never see me again. I wish I hadn't seen that look on their faces. *Hail Mary, full of grace!* Would Letty return the same? How could she? Things were missing and parts of her were gone forever. Hadn't they just gone through this? Fear gripped my parents.

As I am being rolled down the hall with the funny-looking shower cap on and me, already smelling of the dreaded Betadine prewash, I started to pray, "Hail Mary, full of grace…Hail Mary, full of grace…Hail Mary, full of grace…." *Why am I stuck on only this phrase? I know this prayer but it seems that I am just calling on Mother Mary for help.* "Hail Mary, full of grace…" *There I go again. I'm in a loop or am I just loopy?* At least I knew the drugs were working. *Hail Mary, full of grace….* Because I didn't care that I was assaulting myself with questions (*Hail Mary, full of grace…*), was I ever rockin' this shower-cap look! *Hail Mary, full of grace….* Pan left to the parents waving and holding each other as they are suppressing their tears. Cut music. That's a wrap!

It wasn't until after I was wheeled away that my family really began to cry and maybe even mourn for me. They went to the chapel to pray. The surgery was to last a few hours if all went well. This time, someone would come out and tell them how I was doing after a few hours. The hospital staff were very sorry that such anguish had occurred. They had all learned a valuable lesson.

Where am I? I look around. *Oh, the pretty lights again. I'm in the ICU. What did that mean?* I quickly examine to see if my right hand is there. *Whew! Both arms propped on top of the white sheet. Check!* I take a deep breath. *Ouch! Too much, slow down, Lett!* I touch my mouth. *Good, no tube down my throat. Hey, this is better than last time! Ah, there are those beautiful lights, so colorful! Hmm, I must be on drugs still.* I clear my throat, a very faint sound comes forth. *A noise! I made a noise! I hear something. It's going to be okay! I will be able to talk. Man, did that ever hurt! I don't think I will do that for a while.*

The outcome of the surgery was very good. The second scar ended up being about four inches long and pretty straight. When I woke up, I was in intensive care again. I really only stayed there about a day and a half, I think. The surgery was very successful. They had gotten all of the cancer they could see on the right side. It had not been encrusted around any of the muscle tissue. Several of the lymph nodes had been taken out but no muscle tissue. It seemed that the best-case scenario was that the scar would go completely across to the other side of my neck, just below my right ear, but only if the cancer went that far. It should be a clean line that would look like a wrinkle when I got older. I distinctly remember Dr. Schafer saying that. I also remember thinking, *Okay, that's not so bad. Just one side of my neck will look messed up. I can do this.* I am an optimist. Even though I still had all the questions and I was scared because it hadn't worked out that way the first time, I just took him at his word.

Funny thing, I am older now and nothing looks like a wrinkle! People tell me they don't even see my scars, but I do! While they were in there, they manipulated my vocal cords. I made a squeaky noise. There was a very good likelihood that I would be able to make some kind of sound, maybe even talk. Singing was still out of the question because that involved a different area of the vocal cords. All of my other questions prior to the surgery had been answered because I was able to hold up my head a little. It would get stronger with physical therapy. I was alive and I was going to make some noise.

I did not die. The surgery lasted for about six hours. They kept my parents involved by giving them information every few hours. I was back on morphine but they didn't keep me on it for very long. I was happy that my trench coat days were numbered. The second surgery was rather uneventful as far as the surgical team was concerned, but very eventful because the cancer was cleaned out on the right side. I was going get to make sounds, and many of my fears were gone. There were still many unknowns, but for all of us, the hardest part was done. One step at a time.

16

Me and My Guitar

A FEW MONTHS HAD PASSED, I was home from the hospital. It felt wonderful to be in my own surroundings. I remember bending down over my guitar case to unlatch the locks. I felt a bit dizzy and wondered if I had permission bend down. I was very stiff. My neck felt like it had a rod shoved down it with an added crook at the tip. I didn't really want to move it because if I did, it would cause bolts of electric shocks running in all directions throughout my body. The Taser hadn't been invented yet, but I'm thinking it might have been something like that. The surging current would leave me spent and a little out of breath.

I looked like a mummy or a zombie. Actually, more zombie than mummy because I really didn't have the bandages going on. Besides, zombies always seem to have their heads cocked to one side. Why does it seem that every zombie has a crooked neck? I bend down to get my guitar. I am so surprised when I pick it up. It must have weighed a ton (six pounds to be exact), but for me that was an enormous amount of weight. I sat back down on the bed to steady myself and start to move my arm up to the neck of the guitar. It was then that I realized my left arm can't reach. I am in shock! I try again. My left arm just won't make it that far up. How far up? Imagine you are in a sitting position. The distance from your lap to your shoulder is about three feet, and the neck of the guitar is about a foot from your shoulder, so say two feet. Not far, really. But for my arm to move in that direction seemed impossible. I tried and tried. I got it off my lap about six inches, which is pretty good since it hadn't moved that far before. Alas, not good enough to play the guitar. *What am I going to do?* Angry, frustrated, and impatient, I literally grabbed my arm and yanked it up to the neck of the guitar.

Zap! Bolts of shock waves surged through my body. I started to sweat. Tears filled my eyes. From pain? From fear? From frustration? Yes, to all the above. *No tears, no tears! I can do this! Calm down, it's just pain. It will go away!* But it took its sweet time to go away. I looked at my arm, which was still clinging to the neck of the guitar. My thumb is acting as a hook, a nifty trick that I would later employ frequently. As I am waiting for the pain to subside, I now realize it feels like weights are being added to my arm. It is getting heavier and heavier by the moment. *What is going on?* I am watching my arm lose its grip on the neck of the guitar. I am willing it to stay attached. Instead it comes crashing down along side of me. It's as if the arm doesn't even belong to me; it has its own mind. Thud! The bed stopped it, thank God. Otherwise, I was sure it would have landed on the floor. It was dead weight. My arm was my arm but not my arm! I somehow lost control of this appendage. I had no control over my arm! I couldn't stop the thing from crashing down with a thud of dead weight. Searing burning pain. *Oh my God, I think I ripped something! What did I just do? Why was it hurting so much? Maybe I shouldn't have yanked so hard. What just happened?* Okay, my arm is still attached to my shoulder, nothing is bleeding, and it looks the same. *Why can't I keep my arm attached to my guitar?*

I feel my shoulder. *Oh no, another realization.* I can't feel anything around my shoulder. I am looking in the mirror. I see my fingers around my shoulder blade but I just can't feel all of my fingers. I start tapping places on my shoulder and back. Nothing. Dead. Now I am freaking out. *Did I just cause this or has it always been that way?* Tears well up. Spillage, giant drops splash on my guitar. *No! No, don't cry! It doesn't matter if I can't feel my shoulder and parts of my back, everything was still attached. My fingers worked* (well, sort of), *I can do this! Breathe.* I do an inventory: shoulder muscle check, nothing seems torn; arm check, well, it's still attached; finger check, confused but okay. My spirit...my spirits... hmmm! My spirits were bruised and shaken but intact.

As silly as that sounds, I actually did it. I was looking at myself in the mirror sitting on my bed with my guitar flat on my lap. I could see that I was whole yet I have to tell myself that I'm okay. Now a new thing, I lost feeling in parts of my shoulder and arm. *Okay, if I can't feel it, how come I have pain?* Very confusing and mind-blowing at the same time. I don't know how long I just sat there holding my guitar on my lap, fighting back the tears and losing the battle to watching droplets splash on my guitar. "Lett, just do it," I said to myself. My bed was pushed up against the wall. I don't know when I figured out that if I leaned against the headboard, I could pull my knees up to wedge the guitar between my lap and my stomach so I could slant the guitar neck up. I then placed my pillow under my left elbow to give it more height and support. Since I had a range of motion of only six inches with my left arm, I moved my hand toward the neck of the guitar. Although this simple task took forever, I'm finally in position, ready to play. *I did it!* I never thought I could feel so much triumph, only to be dashed against the wall within seconds.

I'm ready. Music here I come! I place my hand in the C-chord position. Wait, my fingers are totally spazzing out! They are not moving in position. *What? Why? Now what?* C is one of the first chords you learn. I had been making that chord for over ten years. *Why won't my fingers make this chord?* There I am with my guitar cradled between my knees. I take my right hand and literally place each finger of my left hand in the correct position. *Okay, God, let's go!* I strike the guitar with my right hand. Ugh, nothing! Well, it really sounded like the very first time I picked up a guitar. Some sound but mostly muted dead strings. That was it, now my chest is puffed out, full of air. I'm holding my breath. I am shuddering, sniffling, and trying not to full-out bawl! My throat begins to ache. It's beginning to feel raw. I either have to cry, breathe, scream, or give up. I am in so much pain, fear, frustration, and shock. I had not expected that! I had been sitting in my room doing nothing, kind of in a funk. I was going to try it. Here is my old friend, my comforter, my guitar. I had it with me in Columbia. It became my major link to home. I played for hours on end to soothe my loneliness and calm my fears. I knew something was wrong with me but didn't know what. I loved my guitar!

I don't want to cry, it hurts too much. I am already in pain from everything I had already done so far. I was also trying to muffle the sound because I don't want my folks to hear. They had already suffered so much for me. I didn't want to add to it. I know they could hear me. It was then I realized that I had perfected a special technique of crying and holding my breath at the same time. I had been doing this in the hospital all along to protect my body from further pain. *Clever, if I hold my breath, the tears will fall anyway and my chest doesn't move a lot!* The method was this; I would hold my breath then cautiously let that deep breath out with great control because if I didn't, the quick release of my breath would then cause my shoulder to fall too fast and usually stop with a painful thud! I guess I lost partial control of my shoulder but never really noticed. As long as I breathed correctly, my shoulder wouldn't come crashing down, causing ripping pain. I learned how to breathe very carefully. I became an expert crier—emotions, tears, silent breathing, and all! Brilliant! There I sat hugging my guitar, silently crying, and holding my breath for as long as I could. As I slowly exhaled, I began to ponder in sorrow as to what might be lost. *Was this it? Am I done playing the guitar?*

My folks knew what I was doing in my bedroom that night. When it was super quiet in my room, they didn't come running over to see what happened. They didn't hear anything or maybe they did. It must have taken every ounce of strength for them to not barge into my room. They could have come running in to hold me, wipe my tears, soothe me, or let me know it would be all right. No, they just let me be. They let me work it out. They gave me time and space.

I'm done crying! I just want to get on with it. As I wipe the tears from my eyes with the back of my sleeve, I slowly take a deep breath, (inhaling carefully) and move the guitar up on my knee. Again, I place my fingers with the help of my right hand in the C-chord strum. I tried to strum again. I tried again and again and again. Finally, it sounded like a C chord. Now I'm crying again, only this time, from success! I really thought I wasn't going to get to play again but deep inside, I knew I hadn't tried hard enough. (Yes, I realize I sound nuts!). I had to try with my whole heart, with pain and tears, and I made it. I knew then that playing was not going to just happen. I was going to have to relearn my fingering. My digits were going to have to reconnect with my brain. I really don't know why that happened. Truly, I did not have brain surgery. I think now it's because there was so much nerve damage, rerouting, and cut muscle tissue that my poor little brain just had to figure stuff out.

Our bodies are a marvel, are they not? After several hours or ten minutes, I was done. It had been a huge night for me. I made the effort to pull my guitar out, something everyone had been waiting for. I perfected my leakage technique for crying and played the C chord! Quite a lot for one evening. I told my folks I was done for the night and went to bed. I never shared my struggle with them. They knew. After many, many hours of reconnecting and practice, I became proficient on the guitar again.

Standing and playing was a new challenge but by then, I was an expert at figuring out how to conquer my body's new limitations. Not inability, just limitations. The thing about standing and playing was that my old strap sat right on part of the incision. At first, since I had lost feeling in that area, it was okay. Solution? Shopping for an oversized shoulder strap and pad, of course. I found the perfect fit with sheepskin on it that sat right over the gaping hole in my neck. It was strange to see the strap there but not feel it. I could feel the weight of the guitar on my shoulder but not the strap. I just had to be careful not to pull or tug too much because then I would pay for it later on feeling like I strapped a ten-pound weight on my shoulder. As time went on and some of the feeling started to come back I sort of became desensitized to the sensations and the electric shocks. I used to call it being zapped. I would envision one of those purple bug zappers they had in the eighties—noisy, crispy sound, and all.

I met my new challenge, and it had been a bit tricky. Through that stage, a new mantra was developed. "Okay, God, lets' go."

17

One-Note Wonder

I TAKE A DEEP BREATH. I'm safe in my bedroom, the door is closed. I'm sitting on the edge of my bed. My music stand is in front of me, ready with my favorite song. With my guitar in hand, all my little fingers are positioned, ready to start playing. I continued to study and relearn my guitar. I am more determined now than ever to play a "mean" guitar. I'm nervous, I haven't sung a note since my surgery. If I followed the rules and did just what they said, there might be a chance I could sing again.

Easy, Lett. You remember what it was like when you first started to speak, it was awful and painful. It shouldn't be like that, right? I mean, I'm talking now. My new voice is weird to me but I am getting used to it. Okay, deep breath. Wait, not so deep, you'll start to cough. Right, okay. Stop stalling and just do it. I open my mouth to sing. At first, nothing came out. *What happened?* I'm thinking "Our Father" but nothing came out. I swallow hard. *Calm. Stay calm.* A little sweat appears on my upper lip. I wipe it away. I strum the A chord. I try again. A squeal, a squeak, a nonmusical squawk came from my mouth. *Ugh, not again! Really?* Tears well up. It was a single flat note and sounded like a cat in heat. It was the most pitiful noise I had ever heard, and it was coming from me! Somebody stop me! There I sat, trying to sing the Lord's Prayer. I'm sure "Our Father" was hiding from this outrageous noise. I know our Lord loves us unconditionally. My voice doesn't depend on that, but that sound would have made anyone cover their ears! Leakage! I cover my mouth in disbelief. Almost like a little child does when a burp passed from their mouth in surprise. I'm holding my breath. What did I expect? Well, I guess I thought I was going to start singing as soon as they said I could. Otherwise, why was I so surprised that that noise came out of me.

I can't believe it. I'm talking! People can understand me now. My voice isn't a whisper. It isn't so raspy, so hoarse, or so painful to listen to. They gave me permission. I followed the rules! I didn't try to sing once the whole time. Plus, whose voice was that? That's not my voice; it's awful and so very low! I sing high, not this bellow that's coming out of me. More tears are now streaming down my face. My heart is breaking. *I thought it was going to be okay, that I would be able to sing. Maybe it's the key. Maybe I need to find something easier to sing.* But, really, the first three notes of the song are the same and the *fourth* note is just a little bit lower. *I should be able to hit the fourth note, it's lower! It's just like the "Happy Birthday" song. How easy can that be?* No, it wasn't that easy, and it wasn't the key. It was me. I frantically kept turning pages in my songbook, trying to find anything that would sound like it was supposed to. You know, like if you are supposed to sing an A then it comes out as A, not a C-minus with a demented pinky! I tried to sing the first note to any song. I was desperate. I start rummaging through the pages. Finally, I think I'll start at the beginning of the book. "Abba Father," "Amazing Grace," "Be Not Afraid." *Ah, that's a good one. I'm petrified! Ugh! Nothing, it's hopeless. My voice is gone!* I put my guitar gently down on the bed. Tears are flowing but there is no sound. I have mastered crying by tears, only this time, I do take a deep sigh. I'm so sad. I stare at my music book. *Nothing.* I'm crushed, dashed against the wall. I'm just sitting there, staring and letting the tears flow. I'm pitiful, wallowing in a sea of tears and sorrow. *I give up, I'll never sing again!*

Really, did I just say that? Do you believe that? No, I didn't believe that. My voice is a muscle and my muscles are weak. *I need to strengthen the muscles I have to make them stronger, then I can recover my old voice. Right? Right! It was just like my arm! I need to work it out, practice, warm up, and gargle. Wait, gargle? How do I gargle if I can't tilt my head back? Okay, I'll figure that out later!* I tried again. After a few times, it wasn't good, but at least I didn't sound like a banshee.

After a few more tries, I mastered a one-note range. Ta-da! It wasn't much, but it was *my* one note, it was the correct note, and it was not flat. It was weak and thin but defiantly doable. I blew my nose, spent, exhausted, and troubled by the unexpected emotional roller-coaster ride. *Would everything be like that now?* I left my room and went to my folks who were in their favorite spots in the living room. I slumped on the couch next to my dad. He put his arm around me, held me close, kissed my forehead, and said, "It'll come." Tears leaked again but this time, because I knew he was right.

I never did recover the second soprano that I was, but I have had many wonderful years of singing alto and now tenor. I call myself a talto, just to give my voice a label and because it's funny. But it's mostly to laugh at because what am I going to do? Not sing? I am not a lead singer, that's okay. But man can I make up harmonies! This was something else I realized. If I sang low, I could sustain a note and keep it accurate. That's a good thing. That means you can tell what the song is by its melody. "Happy Birthday" sounds like "Happy Birthday," not "Mary Had a Little Lamb" and "Twinkle, Twinkle, Little Star" mixed together. I found I couldn't sing the melody or the main part of the song unless I sang it an octave lower, which can be a good or bad thing but definitely another story for another day. As the year went on, I acquired some tricks for my voice. I learned to listen for where my voice would fit into different parts of the song. If I overdid it, it would hurt or even cause throat cramps. I found, like learning to breathe for my new crying method, that I had to learn to sing for my new vocal method.

Thirty odd years later, I am learning to embrace the soulful woman in me. Just imagine the deep, rich tones of Mahalia Jackson singing. She moves your soul, she touches you with such emotion you may cry. I may never accomplish what she did with her voice, but I can pray like she did and strive to reach that soulfulness. Some roads take longer to complete than others. I am definitely a work in progress. After all these years, I am finally getting used to my low, tenor voice. I am not ashamed of my voice. Well, maybe a little, like when the director sends all the tenors off to learn their part and she says, "Okay, boys, go off and learn your part." I would shuffle off only to find that what was high for them to sing was perfect for me! I gave the tenors strength. Me! I can hold those notes and really have fun with it. The guys are almost used to me being there with them. Sometimes I will sing alto but that is more challenging for my voice, and in almost every alto part there will be notes that I can't hit. I mean, nothing will come out. It is very weird to open your mouth and not have a sound come out. Now, after all these years, I know my range so I don't push it too much…well, maybe just a little.

I can't even remember what my voice used to sound like. I still look at it as a regift from God. It works very well for group singing and great at leading children's sing-alongs. I still panic when I have to vocally lead a mass. Sometimes the key of the song is too high and I can't hit the note. That makes things a bit challenging. I almost always have people singing with me. They know my situation and carry on. It is humbling to have to admit it to new people who come along to sing with me that I can't. They must sing when they are supposed to because just maybe, that will be the time my voice goes on strike. Lucky for me, my calling was to be a teacher, and my voice came back strong enough for me to carry through. I have been in several singing groups, even made a few record albums, tape cassettes, and CDs. That was for fun and mostly so people could sing along with us. I do feel blessed that I can sing on pitch, sing my harmonies, and lead a song with my guitar. It has been a wonderful gift God has given back to me. I plan to use this gift until I physically can't anymore.

Lately, I have been wondering how long I should keep doing music ministry, whether I wasn't getting too old and should move over and let the kids do it or was God calling me to keep doing this. Here is another gift I received when I saw the documentary film, "Forever Young". It was a wonderful film about seniors going around singing until the day they died. It refreshed my purpose and dedication to singing. I decided to share what I have for as long as I have it. I love to sing and play my guitar. I feel closest to God when I do it. I feel the Holy Spirit rush into me, filling my heart, my mind, and my soul. What a gift! That's why I still do it.

18

Do, Re, Even Me

SOMETHING WAS HAPPENING TO MY voice, it sounded like there were two of me. I started to freak out. This strange, double-pitched noise was coming out of my mouth. It wasn't singing. What it was, I didn't know. I began to sweat. I think that the "Twilight Zone" and the "Outer Limits" just merged into my reality. *Man, I'm losing it!* Here's how the first vocal twilight zone began.

I was already exhausted before we really started singing. Joe always had us warm up in the hall prior to mass. We went over everything. The adage was "Practice, warm up, then pray." If you missed a step, you wouldn't be praying at mass. You might even slip into a performance mode, which is something you are never to do at mass. We would get to the church hall around 8:30 a.m. to get enough time to sing every song and fix anything we needed to. A special mediation song was sung after communion and was always the highlight for us. The song always had a special message for the congregation and would emphasize and reflect the readings for the day. We took great care in our selections. If we had a soloist, that would be the spot.

We were forever working on the praying aspect and not per-formance part, a very fine line. Our meditation songs were always the latest tunes on the christian hit parade. Perhaps it would later become part of the congregation's repertoire. We would spend the most time perfecting these songs. Our practice in the hall was always done standing, allowing us to open our diaphragm as we warmed up. Joe was meticulous about this. We were to stand by the group member we stood by in church. By doing so, this would allow us the chance to hear the person on your left and right. If you couldn't hear them, then you were too loud. We would work over, over, and over on blending until we were one voice. I have to say this about Joe, in addition to his natural ability and musical training, he also had a great ear. He really helped us pull it all together. We didn't call him the dictator for nothing! By the time we ended our warm-up, I was really drained. My body was screaming "Go home!" at me. Did I drive there? I don't remember that part. I kind of think Lorraine came and got me. That seems like something she would have done. She was always going out of her way for me. I was shaking a bit and trying to hide it. I couldn't ask to be taken home because that would mean someone would miss mass. I wouldn't do that. Why I didn't sit for practice was just me being stubborn. I wanted to show my friends I was strong and recovered. I could do this. However, getting up early, getting dressed and ready to go to church, and standing for forty-five minutes before mass cost me tons of energy. It would be a while later before I learned to pick and choose activities due to my energy level.

After the warm-up, we would walk up this huge, steep driveway to get to the church. If I haven't given you the impression that I am stubborn and prideful, then please let me just say it. I am stubborn and prideful. When my friends offered to carry my guitar and music bag up the hill for me, of course I refused. "I can do it! No, really, I'm fine." I wasn't fine, I wanted my bed! I wasn't even sure if I could make it through to the end of mass. Every ounce of strength seemed to have left my arms and feet. Walking up that mountain took everything I had. I was winded and gasping for breath. When I finally made it to the top, I had to stop to wipe the sheen of sweat from my brow and catch my breath. Man, it was only a driveway, for crying out loud! As we were ascending, everyone was causally walking in a group around me and passing me by so it wouldn't seem too obvious that they had been watching me and protecting me. It really was funny to think that nine people could slowly walk up a steep, twenty-foot-long driveway and seem relaxed and carefree. Usually, we would just plow through the driveway and be done with it. Of course I realized what they were doing, but I was way too busy trying to keep up the "I'm doing just fine" masquerade. I must have looked pretty pathetic because Lorraine just yanked my music bag out of my hand with disgust, frustration, and pity. Then Tom gently took my guitar. We still weren't at the church yet, and I didn't even care. Nobody said anything. I stopped and calmed my racing heart and burning lungs. Pat Fanno, the comforter, just stood there with me and waved everyone on.

Everyone seemed to have a role with me. I don't believe they had doled out duties, but everyone just knew what to do for me and when. I was on the verge of coughing. *Breathe, Lett, don't lose it. You can do it! Calm. Calm.* The attack would have stopped the whole show right then and there. My folks would have been called, and I would have gone home immediately. When we finally did get inside I sat down, shaking and sweating, in a small room where all of the equipment is kept out of sight from the main part of the church. Pat wore the look on her face as she handed me a glass of water. The looks had begun in the hall while I was bracing myself for the climb up the driveway. I didn't care, I sat there while everyone else dutifully set up for mass in silence. As more people came in, they were stopped by the sheer silence. They looked at me and my ghastly color and would do that large open-mouthed whisper thing, "Is she okay?" I heard them, I saw them. I didn't care. I wonder why people think they can't been seen or heard when they are doing that. I was drained.

Prior to mass is always a very busy time, everyone had a job to do. We had only so much time to set up music stands, microphones, cords, and tune up our instruments, all placed and ready to go by 10:00 a.m. Again, my friends came through. Someone got my music together, others tuned and placed my guitar, and two little angels had water and a chair ready for me to sit on during mass. Our service would last for about an hour and a half. It should be mentioned that our group would only sit during the homily, which was at least thirty minutes into the start of mass. We would remain standing for the rest of mass, which was another forty-five minutes, a really long time to stand even if you are well and strong. As we got closer to ten o'clock, things really got very hectic. There was lots of movement and noise. Without me doing my job, we had fallen behind. No one asked, "Hey, Letty do you...would you...can you...?" No, there was no time for that. They weren't going to ask me, they just did it. Silence. Everyone is busy and worried. You know, that kind of quiet, like the elephant in the room. Point made! Letty is stubborn. Just do it and don't ask.

Maybe this was a bad idea. I just might not be ready to do this. I should go home. Even my makeup has melted off. I was as white as a sheet, which is pretty white if you are as tan as I am. *Everyone is going to look at me when I walk in the church. I don't want that kind of attention! No, I'm okay. I just need to rest a bit.* I can reapply my face powder and put on fresh lipstick. I think I even have some blush. *I need to go to bathroom. Oh no, I have to get all the way to the bathroom to do this! Come on, Lett, get up. Look normal!* The looks—*I wish they wouldn't do that. Ugh, it's always the same glance. I wish they wouldn't do that!*

Finally, someone other than my group broke the silence, "What's wrong? Are you okay?"

"I'm fine (*yeah, right*). I just need to go to the bathroom and put some lipstick on." The new unspoken rule was in place. *Don't ask, just do it.*

This time, it was Kathy's turn. All of a sudden, she needed to go too. *How did they know their jobs?* Okay, we left. It was a good thing she came with me as my knees were shaking. She stood very close by, ready to grab me if need be. In the bathroom, I was a little shocked to see my reflection. I looked dreadful, pasty, and pale. I pulled my powder out to cover up the nice shine I had going on. I think it clumped as there was so much sweat on my face. Kathy just looked on. I bent down to cup some water to drink and found I was still shaking. *Great! What am I doing? Why am I doing this? What am I trying to prove? God, help me get through this if it is your will. And God, I hope it is your will 'cause I don't want to pass out!* She handed me a paper towel, and we left in silence.

While I was in the bathroom, a conference had been held. Someone needed to tell my folks that I was forcing myself to do this, that I was weak, and should go home. Donna went to talk to them. They came up with a plan. They didn't want me passing out during mass because aside from the commotion, I could get hurt. As I am entering the room, Joe grabbed both of my arms and squares off with me, he's two inches from my face "Letty, can you do this?" A bit dramatic, but that was Joe's way.

I heard that desire conquers fear. Okay, there must be some desire going on here! I assured them all that I was okay. Yes, I confessed I was shaky, nervous, and a bit afraid. Everyone kind of laughed. Finally, it had been spoken. I think once the fears are out there, it makes it easier for people to deal with. I guess it did for us. I assured them that if I needed to leave, I would ask someone to go with me. I said, "Besides, Lorraine is five foot eight on my left and Pat is five foot two on my right. They would be right there to catch me."

Everyone sort of did that nervous laugh again then we circled around for our prayer, which always calmed our spirits. I sensed them storming the heavens with their prayers. I began to feel better...not great, but okay. I could do this. I would swallow my pride and use that chair. I took a shaky deep breath. Pat squeezed my hand. "Showtime."

Wow, it had to be done! I had to have a first time back but was I ready? I really put my friends through a lot that day. I'm sure that their prayers included me getting through mass and not collapsing in front of everyone. I made it out to take my spot. *There's my family. Oh no, not tears!* People were standing, clapping, and crying. Again, another fanfare of applause from everyone. I waved. My voice was shaky, raspy, and very tight. I really couldn't say much. I whispered a meager "Thank you all so much." I was having trouble breathing. The lump in my throat was so large it hurt. I was shy. Me? I just wanted to crawl away. That was a real phenomenon. I looked to my friends, the ones who had just helped me get to that point. They all had tears in their eyes. Kathy and Pat Fanno were actually crying. I was so humbled that day. It was incredibly overwhelming to feel such love and pride displayed from my ten o'clock congregation at St. Pius X. They all felt so proud as though they helped get me there. I was their miracle, their proof that prayer does work. I took that responsibility very seriously, another reason I had to stay and sing that day. The word was out, I was coming back to the church to sing. Many had come especially for me. They wanted to celebrate the occasion with me and my family. It was a very big deal. I was a big deal...well, not me, my cure.

Our opening song was "Though the Mountains May Fall" by the St. Louis Jesuits. It was on our album. *Okay, this should be easy, just sing and play along. No problem.* It's a happy, upbeat song with a catchy beat. "Though the mountains may fall and the hills turn to dust..." *Oh, that could have been me—dust.* "and a shelter for all who call on his name." *Sing, breathe...wait, this a happy song. Why am I getting choked up? Breathe! Hold it together, kiddo. Mass just started. Oh no, my voice is gone!* Pat looks at me. *Fake it, fake it! You're on the second verse. Almost done. Right after the Gloria, you can sit down, regroup, and drink some water.*

My eyes cleared up. I saw my folks watching me like a hawk. Dad was ready to pounce on the altar and catch me. I don't think they were too much into the mass. But I don't think God minded at all. How could He? Father Kulleck's booming, off-key voice came barreling through. "Everybody sing", and he swings his fist upward. He was in rare form. We all laughed and just kept on singing. *Thank you, Father Kulleck.* All eyes are off me. I sigh with relief. *I'm good, and you're a saint!*

We finally finish what seemed like the longest song of the decade. Fr. Kulleck welcomes me back again. *Wait for it...wait... okay, not too bad.* I give them a little crooked smile, and we move on to the rest of mass. I think I ran through every emotion and even made some up during mass. I was sure the chair was yelling at me to sit in it. Was I hallucinating? Maybe, but the chair did quiet down after I sat it in several times during mass. Mass was exhausting but great. My shoulder, hand, and arm did okay. When it got tired, I did the thumb-hooked-in-hip thing. I must have adjusted my strap a bazillion times. I did fine for the first hour and fifteen minutes, and our meditation song was coming up. This was always our favorite part, where we could sing the message for the day to the congregation. We were going to sing "You Are My Sons" by the Dameans. It was the congregation's favorite and ours too. My voice was okay, it held out. I was tired but saw the end coming, maybe about fifteen more minutes if Father didn't make too many announcements. I was on the home stretch.

We started the song. Back then, this was one of the harder songs to play. I was okay. I practiced it a lot, and my fingers were gliding over the frets. No big deal. Then we started to sing and break out into our harmonies. I begin to sing this wonderful song. "Before the sun burns bright..." It was the same song Joe brought in the hospital on his tape player, the same one that had made me cry in the hospital and my sister cannot listen to without tearing up some thirty years later. I start to feel everything tighten up. I don't want to cry. I can see Mom and Dad and Deb are already on their way to a crying fest. Their dam is finally breaking. It has been such an overwhelming time for all. I take a deep breath. "and rivers flow..." *Hold it together, you can make it.* "I called you each by name..." I keep singing. *Wait, what was happening? Was that my voice?* It was two voices, a high and a low. *How was I doing that? What was wrong? What did I do? Don't cry!*

Somehow my voice split, right out of science fiction. My voice had two different pitches. This had to do with the folds they made on my vocal cords while I was still in the surgery. I was doing the Tibetan Gyuto Monks' throat-singing thing and didn't even know it! The sound wasn't permanent but I didn't know that either. I thought I had really done something wrong and pushed too hard. I feared that when I would try to speak or sing again, I would not have a voice at all or it would be this creepy two-pitched droning thing.

I remember getting hot and sweaty again, thinking, *This was it, I was done for. No more voice.* I pushed too hard. I had been too obstinate about wanting to sing. *Okay, calm down. Did anyone hear that?* Nobody is looking at me, it must have been really light. They are all still singing, nobody stopped. There are no looks. *Okay, so maybe they didn't notice. Take a deep breath, swallow gently, and clear your throat. Sing!* "No longer, be afraid..." *Nope, it's still there. I did it now! Why am I so stubborn? Don't look panicked, keep mouthing the words.* Well, at least I can play this song and my fingers are working. "You are my sons..." I waited a bit. *Breathe, rest until the next verse, clear my throat again. Swallow, breathe, okay, calm, calm.* "My love will never end." *I did it! It's okay? Thank you, God! My voice is back. But wait, will it happen again? Will it stick? Will I lose my voice completely? Maybe I shouldn't ever sing. I mean, if I want to keep talking and teaching, I need my voice. I am being selfish. I should give up singing. I can just play the guitar. That's okay. I can really concentrate on learning how to play better. I shouldn't be greedy. I should be happy with what I have. I am back with the group, I can play. No, wait…God, I want to sing! What am I supposed to do? Halleluiah!* The song ends.

In reality, I pushed too hard. In my longing to avoid crying, that tightening feeling was just that, a tightening of my vocal cords. Since the doctors fused them together, the cords had slightly overlapped, causing the double voice. I just needed to relax, they would return too normal. Even now, I will get the split voice, usually when I am tired, tense, or whenever it wants to. I just stop singing, swallow, wait, and then resume singing. I really don't miss too many beats, and no one notices. I still wonder if one day my voice will just give out. It may. It is weaker, lower in pitch, and more limited in range. It gets tired more often than not. As I continue to sing, my higher notes are completely gone now. It's as if I hit a brick wall and that same flat note comes out or sometimes nothing comes out. That one does bother me still. But, hey, it's okay. I have had a great run. I will just keep on singing until it does stop. I am forever grateful that I have had all these years with any kind of voice. This has also been one of the many miracles that I love sharing.

After the mass, my friends and family whisked me away. Someone grabbed my guitar, another, my music. They even used the side door so I wouldn't have to walk so far. I was packed into the car and asleep before I got home. It had to be done. The first time was over. My voice did the split thing many times after. It always scared me but never as much as the first time.

19

The Comfort of a Constant

IT'S A PASSION NOW, A mainstay, something I can always fall back on. It will forever be a part of my life. It wasn't always that way, but it is now. My life would be so different without music. It is my constant.

I wake to the new sounds of the day. The morning whispers float from the living room like a song. Mom and Dad are sipping their morning coffee and discussing their life events: money, kids, health, vacations, money, kids, and themselves. I don't know, I was just a kid. What I do know is that they would do this every morning for their whole married life. It's what my mother missed the most when Dad died. That had been her constant.

This is how I would wake up sometimes, I would just roll over as the murmurs lull me back to sleep, only to wake up to hear a different topic. I hear the clicking of the mugs on the coffee table and Mom and Dad talking about their world in quiet, hushed tones so as not to wake us. That was my growing-up life, the "all was well" signal, and my childhood constant.

In order for a comfort to become a constant in your life, do you have to recognize it as that? Must it have a name? My friend, who unexpectedly became a widow, told us that we, the ten o'clock music group, had become her constant. She could always rely on the fact that we would be at my living room with music spread all about, laughing and singing and just getting ready for Sunday mass. No matter what happened throughout her week, we became her haven. If life became too overwhelming for her, it didn't matter because we were there for her, not just in song.

Christian music had always been there but I never knew that it was the thing running through my veins. It was the music that did it for me. Was it the fact that my guitar was my steady companion on my adventures in South America? Just holding it brought me closer to home. Or maybe because I had to crawl my way back to my guitar and learn to sing with a different voice? Was it God's way of letting me and others see the miracles He worked on? Or could it be that there had always been a guitar leaning on the wall ready to be played by my dad during my childhood? Either way, music has been a companion in my life, especially now on this journey. It is a steadfast comfort that remains with me to this day.

I know that my heart soars and literally skips a beat when we are in perfect harmony! It is the creation of the fifth voice when there are only four people singing and you can't distinguish one voice from the other and when breath control, volume, rhythms, and understanding of the song are as one. Then it magically happens, an additional voice (a new voice), it does not belong to any one of the singers, it is a true blending of their voices singing together. The fifth voice is unique to the four who are producing it, and only those people singing can create that sound. Four other people may produce a fifth voice but it wouldn't be the same voice. This is that feeling I long for. This is that aha moment.

Have you ever been brought to tears from a song or piece of music? Remember when you would go to a concert and leave exhausted, excited, and exhilarated? Was it something in the performance, the lyrics, the progression of chords, and the harmonies? You might even find yourself crying. You don't even know why but something has stirred your heart. It's because you were transcended by the music. Your whole mind, heart, and soul just received it all. It had rocked your soul to the very core. At times, it has become so exhilarating I can hardly breathe. That feeling is so powerful. I crave it.

I will take it one step further. Since I am usually praying as I sing, this leads me to my closest moment to Christ. It's how God gets to me. Bam! Right there and then, nothing fills my heart with such overwhelming joy, vulnerability, and intensity as when all the elements of music come together to sing His praise. Wow, I get to do that! Me, with my limited, mediocre range, and lower-than-the-gutter voice. I have come to realize that God doesn't care how we sound, just that we sing. We all need constancy in our life, something we can count on, rain or shine. My family is that for me but also my music. It's there, my passion. I just have to go and pick up a guitar. I see and accept the loving constancy music has become in my life. I think maybe, just maybe, I'm finally getting it.

20

Adaptations, Adjustments, and Alterations

Is THIS WHAT THE DOCTORS were talking about when they said there would be an adjustment period? I just never figured that surgery on my neck would affect so many routine and mundane activities in new and different ways, like raising both hands over my head or slapping my arm on the water when I try to swim like a regular person.

As I began to navigate regular routines for the first time since the surgery, I was shocked and surprised trying to negotiate these firsts. I found myself having to adapt, adjust, and alter everything, like going to the bathroom, taking a shower, making a sandwich, drinking a soda from a can, making my bed, getting dressed, and driving my car. It seems that the firsts were always happening as if I never accomplished them before, making me feel like I just got dumped in the middle of a foreign country without my phone, a guide book, a suitcase, or my makeup! Why didn't I ever think about these activities until they were happening, going to happen, or just happened?

Some things I didn't even realize I couldn't do until I went to do them. My life did not end nor was there any blood shed when I couldn't raise both arms over my head. I still swim, it might be splashy or look a bit odd, but that doesn't really matter in the scheme of things.

~My Aching Neck~

I had what might look like a valley in my neck. The valley was created by my jaw and collarbone with only a thin layer of skin stretched across the valley floor. What should have been muscles were now a deep void of negative space. The surgeons literally pulled the skin from each side and sewed it back together. They hadn't taken the muscles directly from under my chin so I could still feel that part of my neck. Also, the exterior tonsil area was left untouched. Other than that, it's merely a thin layer of skin, neck, and collarbone. The feeling of this area is the strangest part. It feels as though it's not part of me, a foreign substance or a placeholder until the real thing comes back, but it never will. In the beginning, it almost felt like leather to me, thick and hard. It did not feel like my skin. When I would feel my neck with my fingers, my brain would not register the sense of touch around my neck area. I mean, it was there but not there. The repaired wiring system had created numb patches all across the lower left side of my face, neck, shoulder, and back area. I would sometimes sit in front of a mirror touching parts of my face and neck to see what I could feel. I would even go as far as creating a game with my friends and family saying, "Oh, I will close my eyes then you touch the area and let me see if I can feel it." I failed every time. It was very peculiar, like my own twilight zone!

If someone pats me on the left shoulder, it takes a few seconds for my brain to tell me, "Hey, someone is touching you." After thirty odd years, it still surprises me when that happens. The feeling on my neck and shoulder area will always be one of several sensations ranging from nothing at all to a tingling, electric shock or a dull muscle pressure below the skin. It's just the most bizarre thing. That thin flap of skin on my neck was so tender, I still gag when I clean it.

I started cleaning the area not with soap and water, but with alcohol, like the nurses did in the hospital. I would moisten a cotton ball or Q-tip and gently swab the area, expecting to feel the coolness of the alcohol on my skin. When I felt nothing, I thought I had missed the area, but that was impossible because I was looking right in the mirror. I tried again, only to realize for the first time that I had lost feeling in my neck. There were parts of my neck that I could feel the wetness of the liquid and other parts as if nothing was there, like the area was dead. Nothing. No feeling! On went the cotton ball, then off, and back and forth. I just couldn't believe that I had lost feeling. *Wow, how long would it be like that?* Not realizing that I had put too much pressure on the area, I would start to gag or cough. I was going to have to learn a whole new procedure for cleaning my neck. After weeks of dabbing and swabbing and mastering the technique, I finally attempted soap and water in the shower just like a regular grubby person.

Since I always had to remember that I had to budget my energy and choreograph my smallest movements, I needed to plan ahead, which meant on the days I washed my neck, my hair was put on hold until the next day because I just wasn't strong enough yet. The trick was to build up enough energy to the wash my neck and include cleaning the rest my body during the same wash cycle. I already learned that my left arm only reached up enough to get soap in my eye, and since getting soapy eyes was not the goal, I started to develop a new cleaning strategy. I would place the washcloth in my left hand, get it soapy, and then move the cloth over to the right hand for cleaning. To this day, I simply hold my breath when washing my neck. Scrub, gag or cough, and keep scrubbing, rinse, then move on. I remind myself not to dwell on the sensations. They will pass, and I won't die from a clean neck.

As years passed, my adaptations, adjustments, and alterations became second nature. I accepted the fact that this had become a life-changing event and some things would never be the same. But I realized that some of these things were so small and almost insignificant that a minor tweak was all that it took. I just had to deal with it, suck it up, and move on.

~It's My Bath Time~

I had not realized all it took just to get in the shower. I had to maneuver the whole thing by myself. I had finally begun to dress and get out of my pj's, which is a good thing for anyone's spirit. I was making an empowering statement. "Hey, I am getting better, and I don't have to be in my pajamas or stay in bed all day!"

I just can't seem to bend so much. I am stiff as a board, the Tin Man begging for the oil can. I am in my folks miniature bathroom planning my strategy. *Wow, this might be hard! Where do I begin?* I realize that I should have thought this through before I went in. I did one thing right, I had taken in clean undergarments and clothes.

Mom yells, "Honey, do you want me to help you get undressed?"

"No!" I reply, trying my best to sound confident, self-assured, and not frazzled, which I was. "I've got it." *Really, do I have it? Where do I start? If I start with my legs and get stuck, then I am naked from my waist down. If I start at my top and get stuck? Ugh! Okay, just yank some clothes off. I am sweating! Oh god, am I going to pull something, rip something, or do damage to my neck? Is it going to hurt? Maybe I should call my mommy! NO, just do it, Lett!* I whack my elbow on the wall. *Ouch, that's going to leave a mark!*

It was then that I realize just how small the bathroom was. The toilet is a foot away to my left, the wall inches from my right, and the glass shower stall is inches in front of me. My mom pokes her head in, saying, "You okay?"

I'm standing there, sweating and a little panicky, half dressed, knee up in the air, trying to pull my pants off and quickly trying to look composed. "No, really, Mom, I can do it." *Did she just see the drops of sweat dripping from my nose?* I give her a meager smile, indicating for her to shut the door. She does so quietly. My guess is that now my mom is sitting inches from the door, sweating as well, ready to pounce in immediately and save me from myself!

I manage to get my pants off and then my underwear. I still wasn't wearing a bra because the strap rested on my poor little shoulder and someone else would have to hook and unhook it. No, thank you. Not for Ms. Independent! One of my friends told me to twist the back to the front, hook it up, twist it back, then maneuver your arms in the slots, and presto! Your bra is on. I got as far as the twist to the front and presto. I gave up. Who needs a bra anyway? My friend also forgot to mention the fact that she was an A cup and I am…well, let's just say I'm zaftig, as my friend Marilyn would say.

Maybe I saved getting the top off for last because I thought it would be easier. Wrong! Even though it was a button-down and my eye-hand thing had been mastered, there was still the problem of maneuvering the shirt off my wrecked shoulder and arm. See, this was one of those firsts. I didn't ever think about how I was going to take my shirt off by myself. *All right, Lett, now take off your shirt. Good, buttons mastered. All undone! Now just take the shirt off.* I try and do that little shoulder-shrug thing. *Oh, so your left shoulder doesn't shrug so well? Great! Just pull your left arm out of the hole. Wait! My arm doesn't bend as well. Oh man! Stay calm, breathe.* More sweat. *Okay, put the shirt back on and start over but don't button it!* I succeeded on the second attempt. I reversed the process, pulled off the right sleeve first then I slid the shirt off my weaker side. It was a piece of cake! *Wow, I just invented a new clothing maneuver for myself!* I am spent already and I'm not even in the shower yet! I'm soaking wet and I haven't even turned the water on! *Who knew this would be so much work?*

Mom was sitting on the bed outside of the bathroom, worrying what to do if Letty gets stuck, *What if she gets stuck?* I did. *What if she passes out?* I didn't. *How do I get in the bathroom if she is blocking the door?* We never had to find out. I hadn't even thought of how this would affect my poor mom. Resolved, she decides, *I'm going in. I can sit on the toilet. That way, I'm in there just in case!*

Just as she grabs the doorknob, I weakly croak, "Okay, okay, I'm in. I'm in. I won't be long." *I can't be long, how can I be? I have no strength left!* I proudly maneuver my arm up to pull on the faucet. *Thanks physical therapy.* Nothing, it didn't budge. I use my left arm because I was forcing myself to do as much as I could with that arm so it would get stronger. *Am I that weak?* My left arm flops down. *Oh yeah, I guess I'm supposed to guide the thing down.* I'm already flustered by my two attempts, and I see my right arm automatically comes to the rescue and turns the water on. *Whew!* I'm finally wet from water, not sweat. I find myself dumbfounded. *What do I do? What can I do? Okay, Lett, just the basics, hair and privates, then get out!* I have the temperature of the water just perfect. Nothing is hurting. I'm spent but ready to begin. I was not prepared for what came next. I squeeze the shampoo to my left palm. *Hmm, smells good! You can do this.* I take a very deep breath. I go to put the shampoo on the top of my hair. My left hand will not go! I try and try again, nothing. It is not moving! *What is happening? Ouch, I have shampoo in my eye! Great, that's how far my left arm will go, just far enough to get shampoo in my eye? Really? Well, I guess I got the shampoo pretty close and sort of in the correct location, just a few inches off. Okay, stay positive. Don't be crushed, it will get better.*

I don't know how long I stayed like that. I did finish the shampoo job with my right hand. Exhausted and feeling a little teary, both from the soap in my eyes and the realization that I might never wash my hair with two hands again. I do use both arms now. I just figured out how to do it Letty style. I got all the important parts and got out. *Oh no, I have to dry off! Oh, forget it! Am I sweating from the shower or am I just wet?* "Mom, I'm coming out and will get dressed later, okay?"

As I exited the bathroom, my psychic mom saw me and my soapy, bloodshot eye, realizing almost everything that had occurred. She said nothing and led me to bed…well, she almost carried me to the bedroom. I crashed on the bed. A deeply frustrated yet cleansing sigh escaped me. I felt satisfied, worn-out, but clean. I thought, *Ah, my haven! My beloved bed.* She toweled off my hair a bit and rubs lotion up my arms and legs. *Glorious!* I did it on my own—except for all the things my mom did, of course. Tomorrow, I was going to wash that crud right out of my neck! The rest of that day, I just slept a very deep, clean sleep. *Mmm, I smell so good!*

~Flash Forward 2016~

"Help, I'm stuck!" Cold sweat is beginning to trickle down my forehead. Kathy and I are in the dressing room, she is trying on a dress for a wedding. I usually don't purchase dresses because it requires certain gymnastic maneuvers I can no longer do. But let's face it, sometimes a girl needs a fancy dress. Today is not that day for me. I saw a cute sweater I wanted to get. Kathy was in one dressing room; I was in what seems like a smaller version of the same room.

I begin the contortion act with my left arm. Perfect, I banged my elbow on the wall. *How do I do this? Which arm goes first?* I slip my left arm in the sleeve and duck my head. *Wait, I need my right arm through the hole. Okay, it's on.* It's a little tighter than I usually get. This became a regular thing for me, getting clothes a little bigger so I can get in and out of them more easily.

I blow my bangs from my forehead. *Nice, I can dress it up or down with accessories.* I love the color, the price is a steal, and the fit is acceptable once I get it on. I make the decision to purchase it. *Okay, now to take it off.* Not thinking how, I began to yank the thing off. Most women do the "cross arms and pull it over your head" thing. Guys? Well, they just grab the back of the garment and drag it over the head. Me? I don't want to rip it so I begin with my left elbow, Wrong! I pull the sweater over my head with my right arm and tuck my left elbow in, trying to squeeze it out of the armhole. *Stuck! Stuck!* I can't move. Did I mention I'm a bit claustrophobic? There I was, trapped in this wonderful piece of clothing. My left elbow is stuck midway through the hole while my right arm has somehow gotten twisted around the sleeve, and my elbow won't bend because it's over my head. I am completely immobile. I can't move to grab any part of the material! The more I try, the worse it gets! *Breathe, breathe. I'm going to suffocate and be found dead in this one-by-one dressing room in a gorgeous sweater! I can't believe this cute sweater will be my demise.*

"Kathy? Kathy, help!"

She answers, "What's wrong?"

"I'm stuck! Can you come and help me get out?" I try and sound as calm as possible but I know she can hear the panic in my voice.

She chuckles. "I'll be right there."

I meekly say, "Please hurry, it sorta hurts."

The dressing room has a lock! Kathy gets to the door and attempts to get in. "Ah, Lett, you have to unlock the door."

Right? How do I do that? I realize I have to use some other part of my body to unlatch the door. My knee or my foot? Oh, maybe my tongue? No, that's too gross. I wiggle two fingers free from my right hand that's wedged over my head. My thumb is hooked on the seams of the sweater. My left elbow is frozen in the armhole of the sweater so I have to use my entire body to flick the latch up. I grope for the door and bend down to find the latch. I'm getting a little dizzy because my head is under the sweater and I can't breathe or see. Like a pretzel, I contort myself in half. I finally got the latch off after the third attempt.

In steps Kathy. She immediately assesses the situation and is doubled up, with tears rolling down her face, in hysterics. She can't stop laughing. It's one of those guffaws that makes everyone else laugh. But I'm not laughing! I'm sweaty, panicky, and beginning to cramp up. We both realize then that the dressing room is too small for two people. The tango begins. Kathy pushes me into the corner as she opens the door. Cue tango music. She takes a step back. Grasping my two protruding fingers, she pulls me forward, all the while laughing and spinning me around.

I think I'm going to barf! "Uh, Kath…" I say, trying not to hyperventilate.

She tries to control herself a bit. Suppressing giggles, she proceeds to untangle me while asking how I got into such a mess. Good question. Through years of experience, I usually always start with the right arm, pull it through the sleeve, pop my head out, and then just drop the garment down over my left arm. Why I didn't do my learned undressing maneuver is beyond me. Maybe because we were chatting through the walls and I usually shop by myself with no distractions. It's a miracle that Kathy had come to the rescue. Needless to say, there were no headlines of a woman found dead in the dressing room strangled by a stunning sweater. After that, I didn't even buy the sweater. It does make me laugh but well after the incident!

No matter what the situations is, adaptations, adjustments, and alterations will need to happen. Some will come easier than others. Sometimes you need to ask for help. I learned mine through trial and error. Oh and my adjustment period? It's still happening.

21

The Magic Pillow

As I SINK MY HEAD into luscious stuffing and silky smoothness, I fade away. Mom just helped me to bed after my adventurous first shower alone. I have collapsed into a warm, clean, and blissful sleep on my magical pillows.

When I came home from the hospital, pillows were such an important part of my life. My mom took to designing different sizes and shapes. I guess you can say the pillows she made were therapeutic for both of us. In a situation where one feels helpless because there is so little that can be done, a few pillow constructions really helped my mom feel like she had made a major difference in the quality of my recovery. Pillows are fabric stuffed with comfort. They are used for support. Should it be called a stuffed animal with no arms? How many times has this dear thing been squeezed, scrunched, rolled, cried into, and squished to our tummy when we have cramps or been our general comforter? It does the trick. Not only does it support our head and other body parts, it is also used for so much more.

I felt like Goldilocks testing pillows to see which one was just right, feeling for its smoothness and softness. As I began to sleep on my left side, I found out that my face was very sensitive to certain fabrics. If it wasn't the correct texture, my brain would keep me awake, trying to figure out if there was sand on my pillow or if sandpaper had somehow gotten stuck on my face in the middle of the night. Changing pillowcases has become part of my routine just so that I may slip into a spiritual dreamland.

~The ICU Pillow Fortress~

The room is white, the light blinding. I squint a bit and see my body encased in a plethora of small, squishy mounds. *Where am I, and why can't I move very well?* When I become fully awake, I then realize that I'm in the ICU. I have about fifteen pillows all around my body—two on either side of my neck, one by the back of my left shoulder, and one under my left elbow. You get the picture. I am in a pillow palace! Somehow I am comforted by these mounds of fluff. They also seem to be doing some kind of physical aide too. Yes, the two pillows on both sides of my neck were keeping it from plopping over. *Wow, I feel like a Raggedy Ann doll. Who knew? I thought they were just for sleeping.* I later realize that if the cushion isn't propped against my head, it tilts to the side and pulls on the stitches, causing pain and sometimes bleeding. More discoveries were made. Aside from physically lifting parts of my body, my soft and fluffy friends also cradle, nurture, and bring me back to the safety of God's hand lifting me up in the operating room. These little wonders provide so much assistance, supporting without an opinion or a sad look. These marvels could take any abuse and absorb any sorrow or pain without a complaint. I didn't have to worry if I was happy, sad, quiet, or grouchy. All I needed to do was grab and squeeze.

I sometimes think these things are like stuffed animals as I would drag a few of my favorite smaller pillows around with me in the house. One would always find its way under my elbow and another supporting my neck. It seems that to this day when my shoulder is achy, there is nothing like a pillow to give me the support I need. These cushy things were so important that my mom even wanted to include a picture on the book jacket. A pillow! She remembers how important they were to all of us.

I still need help getting my head up when I'm at the hairdressers. There I sit, stuck with my head in the sink, wet and unable to lift it up like everyone else. If my hairdresser doesn't help me up, I'll inevitably grab a handful of my hair and yank my head up. I am not being mean to myself but sometimes it's just faster to do that. It doesn't hurt, it's quick, and is over in a moment. It has been well over thirty years and I still have to do it that way. I also do that when my head slides off my pillow at home.

Many years later when my dad was diagnosed with myasthenia gravis and then a brain tumor, out came the sewing machine, the prayers, and the pillow factory was up and running. Who would have thought pillows were so important?

22

The Torture Chamber

WAIT, WHAT AM I DOING? Why would I drive myself over to physical therapy to endure this? Oh yeah, I want to move better. I feel like I'm at a tennis match, back and forth, left and right, and then right and left again. Searing pain. My eyes are brimming over with tears. Little dots of sweat have formed on my brow, and there seems to be no mercy at hand! I called the first torture, the tennis match. This should have been no big deal but when I started, my neck felt like it had a rod jammed inside. Mobility of any kind was going to be a thing of the past, which meant the therapist had to physically move it, an inch at a time. As my therapist gently moved my chin from side to side, I swear I heard the scar tissue ripping away. Feeling like a bobblehead whiplash victim, we both knew I had tons of work to do. The goal of the activity is to be able to move my head parallel to my shoulder or watch a tennis match and not get your head stuck in one position!

I had zero problems with crying in front of people at physical torture—or rather, therapy. I did have a problem crying elsewhere, just not there. Everyone was crying, praying, groaning, grunting, screaming, and thanking or yelling at God when it was finally over. It's just what you did there. I realized it had something to do with the emotional mess that needed fixing as well. Misery does love company; we were all miserable together, gaining strength from each other. The thing is, if you want to recapture any part of what you once had, you have to go through the pain. The adage "No pain, no gain" is really, really true. I don't remember any of my fellow tortured souls, but I do remember being encouraged by them and me encouraging the newbies later.

My neck had been greatly affected by the removal of several major muscle groups because the range of motion (ROM) of my neck and arms were very limited. In addition, my throat muscles were still pretty weak. If I moved my neck the wrong way, I would start to cough. The only thing is, I never knew what the wrong way was. Then I would get embarrassed as if I was doing something wrong and I should know better. My therapist was going to help me with that too. She said it was all wrapped together and not to worry too much about it.

I imagine I'm on the Swiss Alps attempting to make a snow angel. But something was terribly wrong with her wings. The point was to lie on the floor with arms near my side and palms up then move my left arm laterally up and down. Hopefully, I would be able to get it all the way to the top of my head, creating a lavish wing. No such luck. My left arm had its own will, and flinging to the top of my head was not part of its plan. I still can't make anything that resembles a snow angel to this day!

My therapist would get on her knees, grab my arm, and initially move it little by little—pulling, tugging, and pushing it up. I couldn't stand feeling so helpless. *I should just give up. This thing is never going to move, it hurts so much! How is this going to work if the muscles that make it work are gone? Move, you dumb thing. MOVE!* I remember hearing the voice in my head, willing my left arm to move but nothing, absolutely nothing would happen. That is the oddest feeling. This time, I wasn't on drugs and my body was not responding to my wishes. It was a very new experience and humbling. I knew God was with me so why wasn't he giving my arm a bit of a shove? But there I was, it just wouldn't move by itself, and it hurt. *Don't cry, Lett, it'll be okay.* It felt like someone was ripping my shoulder off its socket. Since I had missing feeling in parts of my neck, back, and shoulder area, how could it hurt so much? Our brains are wonderful things. Sometimes my brain couldn't figure out what it was feeling, pain or no pain. Confusing times for my body, mostly I recall the assortments of pain. It had to hurt a lot considering that scar tissue was being broken down and I began to use different muscles in place of the missing ones which meant the remaining muscles were doing new and important jobs for me. They were literally being stretched to new limits.

Little by little, my brain and arm began to work together. But, my brain would never miss the chance to let me know that it didn't like certain movements. My tears always sprang forth. Thanks brain! I still can't raise my left arm parallel with my shoulders. A few years later when I was all mended, I was outside with my kindergarten class and we were flying mock airplanes with our arms out. Kids always do it. The only thing is, I was always banking left. It was a hilarious sight to see students on the playground playing airplanes, all banking left even when they were turning right! Remember, the kids always copy the teacher.

The last recollection of the many other grueling exercises was the spider crawl. I had to take my arm and crawl with my fingers, working them up and down a wall. *Hmm, up the wall?* When I first tried this, it didn't work. It's as if my command center was offline. I had to remind myself that they did not do brain surgery. It took every ounce of strength I had. It was so hard and painful. Plus, my arm didn't move but two or three inches the first time. This was not just physical therapy, it was also a lesson in humility and medieval torture in the twentieth century. My therapist was always so patient and very handy with the Kleenex box, even if I only got a few inches at a time. It took us a long time to conquer the wall.

I say us because I really felt like my therapist was with me every step of the way. My success was her success. Give in to your therapist, they are God's workout angels. I would never be able to play my guitar and have fun living without her! Now I can finger-climb my arm up any wall with the best of them, straight to the top of my head. The only thing is, if my hand leaves the wall, my arm comes crashing down like a dead weight. Gravity always wins. The gravity thing was the hardest part. I just couldn't keep it up there by myself, I needed a wall or something to grab on to. It seems that even though I was teaching old muscles to do new things, I didn't have the right muscles to keep it up in the air by itself. I can get my arm above my head if I hold it with my right hand, but if I let go, it plummets right down. I can't stop it so when it drops, it painfully pulls on my shoulder joint. It's okay, I have learned a ton of tricks to keep that from happening. Really, how often does one raise both arms over the head?

There is always a solution or a trick you can find to help you out. When I started to play the guitar, it was pretty tricky at first. My arm would get really tired. I finally did work hard enough to develop the muscles to raise my arm enough to play the guitar. I later learned to play the banjo but gave it up because the neck of the instrument was too long and I just couldn't sustain the position for very long. Gravity is a very strong force. It really made me sad that I couldn't keep my arm up long enough to finish playing a single song. The solution is a bantar, which is mix of a banjo and a guitar. You play it just like a guitar, only it sounds and looks like a banjo. The neck is very short, perfect, and wonderful. Problem solved.

I went to physical therapy nearly every day. I really don't remember for how long. I do remember doing the exercises constantly and grunting or crying, depending what exercise she had me do. I remember sitting in my car crying because everything hurt. Not just my physical being, but my spiritual and emotional being. That psychological part of me that realizes it wasn't all going to come back was difficult. I had not expected that. I kept thinking that I should be further along and that I should have been able to do everything I could before the surgery. However, I didn't realize that missing muscle equals missing movement. If I understood then that I would never regain certain specific movements, it might have been a bit easier for me to realize that my body still wanted to work, albeit differently. Some muscles can be trained to do the job of the missing tissue, but not all movement will be regained. In retrospect, I think not knowing that may have been a good thing. I might not have worked as hard to regain total movement. I remember looking in my rearview mirror, just staring at myself and thinking I needed to try harder. *Dear God, help me to not be discouraged. Give me the patience and strength to do this. I know You are by my side. I can feel You guiding me throughout. Lord, I don't want to be a baby, I feel so small. I wasn't expecting this.* As the tears fell down my cheeks, I felt a little better knowing that it was going to be okay. We would conquer this together.

I did my exercises faithfully and perhaps obsessively. It's a good thing I did because I got most of the use of my arm back. Okay, some stuff is not perfect. When I ride a bike for too long, my left pectoral muscle feels like it's going to pop out of my chest. My left arm feels like it has weights on it or falls asleep, but that's okay, I can still do it.

I did my research and found out all the things that could have happened to my left side. My arm really could have been a vegetable. It just reaffirmed all the miracles that were bestowed on me. If you look at my neck—I mean, really look at it—the scar directly under my neck is very thin. The scars on the left side are not so bad. There are chunks of flesh missing from my neck. Now with exercises, things don't stiffen up. My head doesn't really jut out anymore. My shoulders look relaxed even though one is lower than the other, which can vary from day to day sometimes hour to hour. I still get buzzed when someone finds just the right spot. I still have places on my face, neck, shoulder, and back where I don't feel anything. But the skin is supple, moves well, and the color is very good. I have a double…no, maybe a triple chin, and I do not have a jawline on the left side.

My mom who lived with so much pain most of her life would say, "If I'm going to be in pain here or there, why not go there to enjoy new scenery? It's still going to hurt anyway." This says it all to me. Attitude is everything!

23

Average Oddities

A DASHING BLOW CAME TO me when I found out I was average in my reaction to many things. But lucky for me, I have oddities that help break the average mold. Face it, nobody wants to be average all the time.

A tricky thing about my throat was if I yawned a certain way, a cord or nerve or something would feel like it would move and then get stiff causing a cramp on the front of my neck. It hurt so bad, it would take my breath away. I would mentally panic a bit, getting a little sweaty and stuff. The first time it happened, I didn't know what it was. No one was around, I couldn't talk much and I didn't know what to do. Somewhere in the recesses of my mind, I figured it was a cramp. It lasted for about twenty or thirty seconds, which is an eternity when you don't know what's happening or for how long it will happen. I thought for sure I couldn't breathe. I couldn't yell for help, and the pain was excruciating in this newly operated tender area. Finally, who's ever heard of a throat cramp anyway? I rubbed it until it relaxed and then went away. Hot and sweaty, I would just sit there, not really knowing what had just happened. It took me years to figure out how to stop that. I learned that if I was in a lying position and yawned, I would get a cramp in my throat area. I still get it sometimes but now I know how to stop it from cramping up all the way. The main thing is to stay as relaxed as possible because panic makes everything worse. I have a few other things that go on with my body like that. When I mentioned it to a doctor they always made me feel very foolish, telling me, "then don't yawn." Funny, but the doctors never told me about throat cramping or about my floating shoulder.

Since they really didn't operate on my back, nothing should have happened to it, right? Well, they did take out part of the scapulae and trapezius muscles that, in turn, has developed into a neuromuscular kind of scoliosis, which means I have a C-shaped curvature in the thoracic vertebrae (upper part) of my spine. Perhaps with the sternocleidomastoid muscle being cut out, it has caused everything to shift. They sort of rebuilt my neck or streched muscles around. A snip here, a tuck there, it was all pretty fast. If someone were to peek under my skin, they would find a turmoil of spaghetti-type veins and muscle tissue. I am a chiropractor's worst nightmare. Actually, I have been turned away from them because they don't know where to begin or end.

~The 101 on a Radical~

My shoulder blade floats up and down the top of my back because of the missing muscle tissue. When my shoulder is high, you can literally see the scapula poking out. When that happens, it burns. Sometimes the skin is as tight as a balloon. I try to rub it back down but it doesn't really help. I guess I figured if I can rub the cramp away, then maybe rubbing a scapula would somehow push it down. Funny how the brain works. I haven't figured out how to remedy that situation, so I mostly just wait for it to settle down. It makes me tired on some days. The muscles in my neck are whacked out (again, not a medical term). My left arm works, but not as strongly as my right arm as it has limited motion. My head juts out. A complete left neck radical caused the limited motion in my shoulder and neck area. That limited my upward horizontal and overhead positioning, causing a sometimes painful shoulder droop. They cut out the left interior jugular and parts of the scalene muscle. The trapezius, pectorals, and deltoid had all been scraped a bit around the bone.

Scraping is good; cutting an arm off would have been bad. But at that time, I didn't know or realize all that the doctors had done.

What I did know was that there were muscles missing from my neck. It didn't work like before. To me and my twenty-five-year-old brain, it looked really, really terrible! *I look ugly…well, not all of me, just my neck!* Therefore, physical therapy was crucial.

24

A Crushing Can of Soda and a Big Fat Sandwich

JOE AND I HAD JUST gotten out of the pool; he gave me a can of soda with a baby straw. *Ugh, I loathe all straws! How can I loathe a straw? It's just a rolled-up paper tube? Is there such a thing as straw therapy? I think I need help.* He was gone, and I was alone, sitting and sipping. I remember getting this idea of drinking straight from the can. Brazen! I took a deep breath. *Okay, I can do this. It's been a while since I tried. Okay, what should I do first? Just tilt and guzzle? No, wait, I should do those neck things.* I bend my head back. Crack! Snap! *Wow, that's a lot a noise going on in my head!* I checked for pain and tried to touch my chin to my chest by moving my head forward. *Huh, no noise! Good.* But it was as tight as a brand-new piece of elastic. *Hmm, maybe I shouldn't try, I might pull something. Wait, Lett, it won't hurt more than the daily torture chamber!*

I gently move my head forward as far as it will go. I do this just a few more times, eager to see if I can get the last drops from the can. *Okay, God, here we go! I feel so sneaky. Nobody is watching. Good, they won't see the disappointment on my face if I fail again. I feel so bad when I can't do stuff right and then they feel bad that I feel bad. I do need help! Breathe, I can do this. It's just a can of soda, for crying out loud!*

My first time was so rotten for everyone. It was a sunny, Saturday afternoon. We were in the dining room, eating lunch and talking. Joe was there, of course, as well as Mom, Deb, and Mari. I had been drinking from a Coke can pretty well. When I got to about a third of the way down, Crack! My head made a popping sound. *Ouch, ouch, ouch! What's happening? My head is not moving back.* I put the can down. *Testing, one…two…three. Okay, it moves left and right a bit. Up and down?* It moved slightly. *Well, that seems okay. Okay, try your soda again. Ouch, that hurt more this time! What is going on? It won't move!* It was then I realized that all conversation had stopped.

I must have looked like I tried to swallow an entire hard-boiled egg in one bite and then it got stuck. *I'm stuck! My neck froze and it really hurts. What did I just do? All right, I was drinking a soda and then everything stopped. Why do I have a bolt of searing hot pain spreading through the back of my neck? I think I stopped breathing for a second. Should I move? Can I move? Did I break something? Will I end up back in the hospital? A can of soda did this? Wait, what did I do?* I gently try to move my neck. It wouldn't go back any further but did move forward. I tried several times, only to be dismayed and in pain each time. It was stuck and would not move enough to take that last swig! Luckily, the pain ended when I stopped the motion. But the realization that my head may never go back again was heartbreaking and discouraging.

Leave it to my mom to jump to the rescue. After she made sure I was okay, she ran to the kitchen and came out with the infamous straw! Proudly, she inserted the straw into to the can. They were all giving me the look. For a brief moment, there was an added guest at lunchtime, the elephant had entered our gathering. But I couldn't let on that I was terrified, that I would look like I had a rod jammed down my neck for the rest of my life. Crushed yet not wanting to yield to the emotions, I grabbed my soda can, looked at the straw, did a lopsided shrug, and chugged. It was a turning point. We were having such a nice time, almost like a normal lunch. I didn't want to ruin it.

Months had passed. There I sat in the backyard wishing…no, demanding me to master the head-tilting, can-swigging thing! I held the can in my right hand. I took one sip. *Good. Go on, tilt further back.* The second sip was better. *Come on, go for it!* The last drop in the can, the final sip. *Wow, I did it!* It seemed like a million years since I tried to drink the last swallows in a soda can.

In the kitchen, something caught Joe's eye, they stopped talking and began to watch. Joe said he remembered my first attempt and was wishing really hard for my success this time. *Ah, the last drop, I did it!* They came out laughing! I was startled by their reaction then realized they had been secretly watching. We all cheered. My eyes were moist. I think Mom's and Joe's were too. I threw away the straw with great ceremony. I reached a goal. As simple as it was, it was my marker. Now on to the next task.

~My Big Fat Sandwich~

My next food challenge was to conquer a humongous sandwich from Canora's. Since the surgery, eating had become a very big ordeal. At times, it seemed as if my jaw had been wired shut and just wouldn't open very wide. Mostly I didn't like to eat because things would get stuck or slide down very slowly, triggering a painful coughing fit. Eating was just not fun.

A field trip, a field trip. We are going to leave the house. Yes, this is a good idea. I have been in a funk as of late. *Maybe this will help.* As my small gang of girlfriends get out of the car, my heart begins to beat rapidly with anticipation. A new noise! *No, that's okay. It's just my stomach screaming at me, it wants to eat. Here it comes. I picked the perfect picnic table to watch this monstrosity come to me. It's giant, bigger than I remember! And the smell! I think they make the best sourdough bread in San Diego. My mouth is watering in anticipation.* I was ready. My friends looked at me and then at the sandwich. We realized at the same time that there was no way I would maneuver that whole sandwich with one hand, it would fall all over the place. "NO, don't!"

Too late. My friend Deb quickly grabbed a knife and then cut the sandwich in quarters. *Man, is she going to cut the crust off too? Okay, smile. She's just trying to help.* I hadn't mastered the use of folding my arm in a ninety-degree angle yet. Even with my elbow supported by the table, we both knew I couldn't maneuver a Canora sandwich to my mouth. I had to swallow back tears of excitement before I could savor the sandwich. I grabbed a slice of the sandwich with my right hand. I tried to take a bite, only to find my mouth could not open big enough to get the top and the bottom in at the same time! It was as if my jaw was wired or stuck or something. I just couldn't get it open. *Wait a minute, wait a minute! I have been working on this at PT. I can do this. Think like a snake, unhinge my jaw, move the back of the jaw, and open my throat. I'm gonna choke! I'm not a snake. Who am I kidding? The sandwich is too big! Don't cry. Think, think!* I had to put *one finger in my mouth to stretch my jaw, then two fingers vertically in, and finally three digits. You did it, Lett. Now do it with the sandwich.*

I take a bite of what I could get in. *Okay, it's not such a big bite, at least it was something.* I did get some of the sandwich in my mouth. It was delicious. Turkey, sprouts, avocado, smoked bacon, and tomato. *Mmm, juicy!* I chew, savoring the flavors. I start to swallow. It's really not that big of a chunk (about the size of a quarter) *Oh no, it's too much!* I feel the juicy wad sliding and scraping my throat. I begin to cough and cry, partly from choking and partly from frustration. Mostly my friends thought I was tearing up because I was choking. *Control, control. I must have control!* I don't want them to feel sorry for me. I don't want them to feel bad because they brought me here to make me feel better. I stopped choking and crying. To assure my friends that I was okay, I took a second bite. They were watching in anticipation, *I can do this. Relax, breathe!* Everyone relaxed. It had been a really hard field trip. *Stay in control, Lett. It'll happen, just not all of it today.*

Something I learned to master really well was my feelings. Somewhere along the line, I had made a mental list of what were acceptable reactions for certain activities and what kind of attention I could handle and what I couldn't. Cooing and fawning were out! Bad attention. I didn't want anyone feeling sorry for me. As always, a brave face was put on, which meant I could tear up from choking but not show my dear friends that I was crushed inside that I couldn't eat my favorite sandwich like everyone else. I was feeling overwhelmed. *Ugh!* Out came the fork and knife. *Nobody eats a sandwich with a fork and knife, I'm not in Europe or Colombia, for Pete's sake!*

In a way, it was good that I choked because then they would never know how upset I really was. I thought I was fooling my friends. I thought I was showing them how brave I was. Hmm, not so much they knew. Later, they would report to Mom that the sandwich field trip wasn't a total fiasco. We had gotten through the crusty part. We still had fun, and the real purpose was to get me out of the house. Mission accomplished. A new second food goal appointed itself - eat a Canora's sandwich like others eat a sandwich, handful by handful and napkin by napkin. I did conqueror the Canora sandwich. It took almost a year but bite by bite, I mastered the task.

25

The Terminal Ward

I CALLED IT THE DEATH ward because that's what it was. Everyone was sent there to die. I am getting ahead of myself. It was October. I was done with all my surgeries; my arm was good. I was playing and quasi-singing with my group. I was getting ready to substitute teach, and I was still living at home. I was feeling pretty good.

It had finally come, the day to start this new experimental radiation treatment. I was told to report to the top floor at Scripps, La Jolla. There I would say goodbye to my parents and begin the treatment. I would not be able to have visitors until the radiation readings were at a safe level. My mom would have to prepare and do a million things when I went back home. She became my own personal slave. I mean, not only was she taking care of me, but now she was just handed a brand-new, doom-and-gloom list of how to take care of Letty. I got it but didn't get it.

The choice had been made. There was no turning back now or was there? No, this was it. My prognosis was awful. I had a .01 percent chance of survival. The doctors said, "She has nothing to lose. She will most likely die if we don't try this, but if she lives she will be helping other cancer patients in the future. If she dies, she will still be helping us with our research." I guess none of us really realized all the extra precautions that we would have to undergo.

~The Hospital~

Upon arrival to the hospital, I was quickly sent up to the top floor. I think my parents were filling out paperwork because I was by myself. I was told to wait by the nurse's station because my room wasn't ready yet. Not eager to obey, I nervously started to wander the floor. I remember this very clearly. It was a typical hospital floor with the nurse's station in the middle of the ward. There are windows in all the patients' rooms and the floor is lit with both natural and incandescent lighting. Most the nurses are still wearing the typical white garb of their profession with a smattering of new, modern-colored uniforms slipping in. As I started to walk around, I began to read some of the signs on the patients' rooms.

-NPO *(nothing by mouth) What's that?* "Caution, oxygen in use. All visitors must wear a mask and gown. All visitors must check in before entering any room. No exceptions!" *Gown, mask, and gloves required?* This was my favorite, "Keep out! No visitors!" *Oh man, what's wrong with him? What kind of floor was this? No, wait, they were all dying! Was everyone here dying? I am not dying! Am I dying? Why am I here? Am I dying? No, I can't be. Look at me, I…I don't look like them, do I?* I began to perspire and get a bit dizzy. I continued to wander. *Okay, I look banged up but I am strong. I am eating. I am walking. I am not hooked up to every machine there is, like before. Why am I on this floor?*

I find myself back at the nurse's station. Looking up from her work, the nurse meets my eyes with kindness and a smile. I clear my throat, nothing comes out at first. I try again. "Is this is the terminal ward?" I look around, my folks are nowhere to be found. I seem to be having a bit of trouble getting enough oxygen to my lungs and brain. I'm really dizzy now. *Maybe I should be here. I can't seem to breathe very well. Maybe this is how it starts. If you can't breathe, then you go into one of those dying rooms. Wait a minute, Letty.* I try again. "Why am I here?" I didn't ask her the real question on my mind. *Am I dying? Is that why you put me here?* Some things are best left unsaid.

She saw my eyes well up and my lips quiver as I asked the question. She paused and gave me a kind, loving smile again. *Oh god, the look! I AM DYING!* Her response was very careful and wise. Again, a memory etched forever. She said, "Yes, this is the terminal ward. The people here are very ill. Many will not leave this ward alive. You are here because we had nowhere else to put you. Your room is not ready because we need to prepare it for the influx of radiation you will bring to it. We need to take anything out that will permanently absorb the radiation." *Absorb. Wait, what? This is a dying ward, no room anywhere else. I'm not dying! I'm not dying…well, not at this minute!* Okay, that worked for me. I accepted the explanation. It rang true. *Hey, I'm not dizzy anymore, and my lungs seemed to have found some air.*

Ding, ding! The bellhop arrives, the room is ready. "Please take her in." I walk in. Everything is white! White sheets, white walls, and harsh, unforgiving white beams of light. I guess it hadn't really sunk in that no visitors meant no visitors to share the whiteness with. I did have a stack of books to read, a TV, and my tape recorder with the Sounds of the Son record album and a few other cassettes. I was ready for the long haul. My folks appeared just as I was walking the few paces around the room. This would be my new home for a while. They both tried to look cheery, not very good actors really. Bless their hearts, they had already been through so much. This was far from over. The nurses told my mom that she should leave because I had a long day of tests and preparations for tomorrow's treatment. I would be out of the room most of the day. Through suppressed tears, my mom and dad left. I was alone. I unpacked my junk, placed the books by the table, and waited. I sat on the chair, not ready to assume the patient position.

The parade began. One thing I was already used to was the bloodletting. When taking blood, the technician always had a little tray with six or twelve empty vials of various sizes that would clink with an empty ring as they entered the room and clunk out as the full vials left with my blood. "Blood Call", a pint, a quart, a gallon, who knows, but it seemed like it was enough to fill a tub. I was really good at giving blood too. I would try to see how fast I could fill the vials up. With one pump of my fist, it would fill up faster. They later told me not to do that, but I did it until they told me to stop. In either case, giving blood was never an issue. The faster, the better then it was over. Sometimes they took so much that I would get juice and a cookie. Only at first, I couldn't eat the cookie and the juice pulp was too chunky for me to swallow. As time passed and I got stronger, I ate more cookies and drank gallons of juice. Tasty.

I finally got dressed in my gown and sat on the bed. Then I realized my door had its own signs. But my signs were different from the other rooms. These postings were all over the door and walls. Caution, Radiation! Do Not Enter! Keep Out! It meant I would be alone for a week. *I feel so small. I think I'm shrinking. Is this stuff going to kill me?* The signs made me feel very strange, and an awful feeling of doom and gloom swept over me. *I can't believe this is happening.* Stop, do not enter! She is contaminated! *Me? What does that mean? Am I contaminated? Am I radioactive? Will I kill people? Just how sick am I going to get? Am I going to glow in the dark?*

It was as if I had become one of those short movie newsreels. I can still remember seeing the testing of the H-bomb. The scientists cluster together in a lead-lined bunker with very thick, leaded glass windows for viewing the experiment, all wearing protective glasses. Plastered all around the room were the infamous three, large, black triangles shouting, "DANGER, RADIOACTIVE! KEEP OUT!" *Now these signs are on my door!* Overwhelmed, I began to cry. *I want my mommy!* Because of contamination, there was no phone in my room. I asked the nurse to call for me. I'm not sure what she said except that I really wanted and needed her and my guitar. My kind nurse conveyed my aguish, and I'm also sure she said that I was crying and appeared very scared.

Since nothing about this process had ever been simple, another plan had to be formed, starting with getting permission from the doctor to allow my guitar in the room. Would the strings and wood absorb radiation? Since I was young and they just didn't know all the ramifications of the treatment, they gave in. That night when my folks came again, they brought gifts: themselves, my guitar, and some delicious, crunchy Cheetos! Although it seemed like a very short visit, I was so happy they were there. I dreaded what was coming. When the time came, there were lots of last-minute hugs and promises to wave from the window.

When they got out of the building, they had to locate me. Once done, it seemed as if we hadn't seen each other just seconds ago. There was a bunch of jumping and waving. I was so happy to see them I felt like a little kid. They would later drive up during the week just to wave at me, always leaving me with a bittersweet feeling. It was a good thing I was so far up because they couldn't see the tears rolling down my face. I smiled and waved frantically as did they. Feeling alone and literally isolated, I plopped on the bed and started to cry. My mind was racing. *What was going to happen to me? Are they lying to me and I really was on this floor to die? What was I going to feel tomorrow after it started? I heard people say they wanted to die after they started their treatments? Was this that? If I really let go, would I ever stop crying?* More tears. *My poor mom and dad, what was I doing to them? How am I going to do this all alone? Hail Mary, full of grace.* I fell asleep.

I knew my mom wanted to be right by my side for the whole thing. She was leaving me and could do nothing about it. The separation was unbearable. I imagine them walking back to the car with Dad's arm around her, silenced by their tears. I know my mom and she would be praying to St. Jude. *Intercessor of the impossible, give my Letty strength. Let her feel God's presence throughout this week. Give me strength, Lord. I feel so weak.* They drive home in silence, each weighed down by in their own sorrow.

My fears were real. I hadn't been alone for any of this. There were always family, friends, nurses, and doctors. Somebody was always there. Even when I was by myself in the hospital, the door was always open, and there were people milling about. There were always lights everywhere, and the noises became my mechanical comforters. At home, the hospital lights and noises had been replaced with comforting silence and soft lights. Feeling like I had the plague and nobody could be near me, I was now going to be utterly alone. My feelings were raw at times, thoughts convoluted and confusing.

Somehow, I was relating these isolation feelings to my first night back from the hospital. Mom had just tucked me into bed, turned off all the lights, and left. It was so dark and quiet, the stillness was creeping over me like a thick, leaded blanket. *What if my heart stops or*

I stop breathing? Who was going to help me? Where was the tracheotomy and heart pack? Even the whirring of the machines and all my hospital equipment was gone.

"Mom?" She came bounding into the room. *Had she been standing right outside the door?* I tried to sound brave. "It's pretty dark, can you leave the hall light on?"

She tried to match my timbre. "Of course, honey. Do you need anything else? I can sleep in here if you want. We have the trundle bed, remember?"

"No, I'm good (I wasn't). It's okay."

"All right, dear." She tenderly touches my cheek. "I'm just next door." She bent to kiss me one more time and left. She wasn't okay either.

Funny how we lied to one another to spare each of us sorrowful feelings. I don't think either of us slept well that first night. Mom kept creeping into the room to make sure I was breathing; I kept waking up to make sure I was alive! For some reason, my brain was combining these two nights together. Was it the lack of the whirring sound or did I miss the soft light and stillness of my house? Or was it knowing Mom was not going to creep in to check on my breathing? Maybe it was just that I was feeling lonely. Break into the Eric Carmen's song, "All by myself, don't wanna be...."

~Me and My Guitar~

Ah, my guitar! My buddy, my pal, and my earthly strength while in South America. Many long hours were spent learning and practicing it. It consoled me and was one of my strongest links to home. The feeling of comfort as it presses up against me and the vibration of the strings and the melodies floating by have become my constant. Every time I opened my guitar case, the smell of rosewood enveloped me. I can still close my eyes and inhale the aroma wafting over me— it was beautiful, wonderful, and my comfort. My mom also brought up some church music and my favorite Peter, Paul and Mary songbook. I guess paper didn't collect radiation waves because nothing was said about that. *Okay, now I was set.* I had already gone through the trauma of starting completely over on my guitar a while back. I could now make most of the chords, I just needed practice. Being locked up in this room was perfect. I would go through the music my mom sent while sitting on the hospital bed, coercing myself to play. *I'm bored, I think. Ugh, who cares anyway? Just play, Lett. Yeah, but I don't feel like it. Play anyway.* I did. I couldn't even win an argument with myself, my emotions were so mixed up.

White sheets are rumpled around my feet. My knees are bent, propping my guitar against my stomach and chest. My head and left arm are propped on the pillows. I played. The room was stark white, the blinds were white, and they were drawn with slits of white daylight streaming through. Now that I think about it, I should have written an "I'm All White" song. *Was I on my way to the pearly gates?* The door was open to my room. I could see the angelic nurses busy at work. Their pure light glowed, surrounding the station. Not too noisy, sort of a reverent stillness with motion. While trapped in bed, I would always seem to fall back to the same song, "They Will Know We Are Christians by Our Love." It was a sixties tune and upbeat but I had slowed it way down—very soothing, slow, and tender. I mastered the three easy chords of the song so playing it was great practice. It was the picking that gave it a haunting sound, which seemed to lend it to further embellishments. I was becoming a better player again. It felt right.

Closing my eyes, I let the music fill me up. I would take a deep breath and zero in on the cards at home in my bedroom. I would visualize the closet doors, focusing on each card and trying to see who sent it. *I still can't believe that all these people sent me cards.* I let their thoughts, love, and prayers wash over me. My fingers are working wonderfully. I don't even realize I'm playing. The music is there, the serenity is there, and the strength and peace are there. Time stands still. Everything is just fine. I am lost in the moment of prayer. I keep playing the same song over and over. The poor nurses probably wonder if I know how to play anything else. My mind and heart are briefly still. I am in a trance, a meditative peace has washed over me. *Shh, don't sing, you'll ruin it. I feel so soft and cozy right now.* That would have broken the spell, the peaceful feeling. Reality would have set in. I used to be a second soprano, not as high as a soprano but I could hit some high notes. Actually, I still wasn't even used to my new speaking voice, let alone that one-note, flat range I had acquired. When I did start to speak and the hoarseness sort of went away, I sounded just like Kathleen Turner. Wow, now that's a great speaking voice. Raspy with just a hint of sexiness. Alas, I didn't keep that resonance. Unfortunately, my singing was not coming around as well as my playing. It was still a very sad and physically painful experience for me to hear the awful sounds coming from my voice. No, I didn't sing.

I did have another tune I would trade off with. This is something I wrote. It was high-pitched and reminded me of little birds chirping. But mostly I would play the slow, tender song. It seemed to help me the most.

As the days passed, I finished both books, watched TV, played my guitar, ate my Cheetos (they tasted pretty good too), and mostly just stared out the door. I would sometimes wake to find my guitar put back in the case and myself tucked in bed. As I said, the nurses were all so kind. I knew they were watching and caring for me. I was the youngest person on the ward. At twenty-five, I wasn't with the sick kids and teens. No, I was with all the old, dying people. There really was no place for me to go. Alone and yet not alone.

26

The I-131 Day

"MISS ROCHA, GOOD MORNING. IT'S time to go. We must get an early start because we need to monitor you all day," said the really cute orderly. He let me comb my hair and brush my teeth.

He is really cute. I just woke up. What do I look like? "Can I at least have a cup of coffee?" I ask.

"Nope, sorry."

Off we went. I was taken downstairs to the bowels of the hospital. They had a very special room deep, deep in the basement. It was all sealed in metal, just like my vision of the H-bomb bunker. I knew we had arrived because the dreaded radiation signs were posted everywhere! *I had become a newsreel clip!* I was wheeled up to...*Oh my god! This really is a leaded door. It kinda looks like a bank vault door. What is the nurse wearing? Why is she covered from head to foot in a white hazmat suit?* I gulped as she rolled me inside. There we were in this very tiny, dark room about the size of a small walk-in closet. There is a three-by-three mirror on the wall. I sat there for a while, wondering what I should do. I looked in the mirror. *Man, I look awful! My hair is a mess, I should have used a brush. What am I waiting for? Am I going to get an outfit too?*

We didn't exchange words, which is very weird because I talk to everyone about anything. I'm watching as the nurse takes out a long pair of tongs. She reaches over to what looked like a box about the size of work boots. *When did that get there?* I stare in dread at the small lead door as it slowly opened. It could have been a horror movie. We were in a dark room with the feeling of impending doom. The only thing is the door did not creak and my monster may actually be my cure. She then reached into yet another sealed box. *Another box. A box in a box? How many boxes are in there? What is this stuff?* The final box contained a test tube-shaped, dull metal cylinder. She grabbed it with the tongs and placed it on the lead counter top. Still no words. *When does she start to say something? Why am I not talking?* She quickly left the room, closing me in the vault. Silence. *Wait! Stop! You forgot something…ME! What am I supposed to do?*

There I was, all by myself in the dimly lit room. I started to get a little creeped out. *What was happening? Why wasn't she saying anything? I really want to leave and go back to my white room with the bright light. It's very dark and spooky in here. Oh no, something is happening to me! I wish I would calm down. Hail Mary, full of grace…*

Then suddenly, as clear as day, this picture started to develop in my mind. I can see my bedroom closet door covered with letters and the bags of cards on the floor. I remembered all these people who were praying for me. *Okay, breathe.* Peace. *You can do this. Do what? Remember they said you were going to drink this stuff. Ugh, drink this stuff?*

Finally, I hear the sound of a microphone turning on. "Hi, Letty. I'm sorry I didn't say anything to you in there. I'm sure it was a bit freaky, but I knew you wouldn't understand anything I was saying to you through this suit." *Ohhh!* I calmed down a bit more. "Letty, Letty, do you see the cover over the cylinder?"

I look at the lead container and spotted what she is talking about. I guess she can see me through the two-way mirror. *Oh, it's not just a mirror. It's one of those police kind of mirrors. That's not fair. I sure would feel better if I could see her.* I clear my throat. "Yes," I replied, looking at the mirror but not seeing her.

"You have to slide the cover over," she instructed. "Yes, over there is a tiny screw holding the cover in place. Don't worry, it won't fall off." I must have had a questionable look on my face because she tried to calm me. "It's okay, honey, I can see you. There is a very thick mirror between us." *I know, but why isn't it a window? It makes me feel like an experiment and you are spying on me. Wait, I am an experiment and you are spying on me!* It was then that I really started to examine the mirror. It seemed very thick and even had some kind of reinforcement around the seams. *Now there's a question. Did they reinforce the mirror to make sure nothing in the vault would try seep out? Am I in prison? Am I locked in?* I didn't have any time to check because she started talking. I must have looked panic-stricken with the whole deer-in-the-headlight expression. "You're okay, just relax. Put the metal straw in the container and drink it." At first, I didn't see the straw sitting next to the cylinder. *What, drink this stuff? Oh yeah, drink it. What if I ended up like Dr. Jekyll and Mr. Hyde? What's it going taste like?* More panic. *Breathe. Hail Mary, full of grace....* I slowly unwrap the straw. *Okay, slide the cover over. Just do it. Is this stuff going to be on my fingers too?* Little beads of perspiration start to form on my upper lip and brow. Our eyes meet through the glass but I don't know this. I can't see her. She tries to sound encouraging. "It's okay, you can do this."

Breathe! What's going to happen? Oh god, can I do this? What if I spit the magic elixir out because it tastes so awful? Will I throw up? Will it hurt? Am I going to start coughing? Then what? Will they have to stop the treatment? Of course, it's gonna hurt. My throat wasn't all that great yet. I was still choking on stuff, and sometimes food or liquids would slide down in slow motion, which would then cause a tickle effect and a coughing attack. I didn't want to start coughing. Sometimes it was very hard to stop. It always left me breathless and completely spent. I hesitated. *How can I do this? I must be nuts to be trying this thing. Look where they have me. I am in the bowels of the hospital, their deepest, darkest spot. Would anyone even hear me if I scream? Can I even scream? Just look at her outfit, she is covered from head to foot. What am I doing?*

Magic? The Holy Spirit? I pick the second choice. I saw the cards again, all those prayers of strength and peace. They were praying for me because I couldn't pray for myself. Did they realize the power of their actions and how they were helping me right then? Sometimes people think that something as simple as a card doesn't make a difference. I beg to differ. It was making all the difference right then and there. It was giving me strength. *Have courage, you can do this.* I wipe the sweat from my face and dab my palms on my gown. *This can save you. If it doesn't, it will help others. I don't think they would have given me something that would kill me, would they? No, they are trying to save me!* I stared at the three-inch metal container and adjusted the metal straw inside.

She had said to drink it and make sure it was all gone. "Oh, and Letty, try not to let any of it touch your tongue or teeth." *Really? You have got to be kidding! How does one drink anything without that happening?*

In slow motion, I grabbed the straw with one hand and the container with the other. I look into the cylinder. The liquid looks clear and a bit dark. It's not thick or sticky looking. It has a watery consistency. *Deep, deep breath. Hail Mary, full of grace….* I take a drag on the straw. It was so cold my teeth began to ache. *Oh god, my teeth are going to fall out!* That also meant I got some of it on my teeth, something I would pay for thirty years down the line. *Okay, not bad. I'm not gagging, it didn't burn or fizz, and I'm not foaming at the mouth.* It really didn't have much of a taste, except maybe metallic. I take another swallow. My eyes are not rolling back. I didn't fall to my knees, withering in pain. My hands are not grasping my throat. I think I watched and read too much science fiction. I literally recreated the Dr. Jekyll and Mr. Hyde scenario in my head when Spencer Tracy was clutching at his throat. Nothing was happening! I drank it all up, making slurping sounds and all.

She said, "Okay, you're done." *That's it? That was the wonder drug that was going to save my life? Was I going to turn into the Incredible Hulk? Didn't Dr. Banner drink his experiment? No, wait, that was gamma rays.* I touched my arm and no green muscles were forming. *Hmm, I feel the same.* Who would have thought comic books could influence a young mind so much? I hadn't read comics since I was twelve.

They were hoping the benefits of the medication would start as soon as possible, but it was an experiment so, really, the verdict was out and we were all waiting. I went down to the dungeon every day, drinking the wonder toxin for a week. I never did turn into Jekyll or Hyde. I can't say when it started to hit me. Was it that day, that afternoon, the next day? I don't know, and I really didn't care. See, that was part of the effects of the drug. You don't care. Apathy was one of the side effects of the radiation therapy, along with listlessness and lethargy. Kind of hard to battle a disease when you just don't care!

As the days went on, I would go every morning down to the basement and drink the wonder toxin. Every day for several times a day, they would come in and do a reading on me. As the tech guy (not the really cute one) would come in with a Geiger counter, I would just watch him. He never really talked much. He had his little badge reader on him, indicating how much of a hurry he had to be in. He would quickly write the info down then off he would go. I would stay in my room and just lie on my bed or sit in the chair. I was mostly in a "I don't really care what you're doing" phase. I just wasn't my talkative, curious self. Again, very much not who I am.

I was a study group of one. They were working out dosage and effects and everything. I really was the first person of my age to get this stuff. Literally, one in a million! I had books so I read them. The first book I read was "The Amityville Horror." That is a scary book! People say they had nightmares from it. I can remember sitting on the bed yawning. *Oh yeah, that's scary.* As I was saying it, I was bored stiff. Nothing fazed me. I would read something and think, *I should be scared here. Why don't I want to stop reading the book like I did with The Shining? Come on, Lett, get scared!* Nothing. I just kept reading as if I was reading a children's nursery rhyme. When I read "The Shining," I ended up doing it during the day because it kept me awake at night from fright. This book was supposed to be even scarier. I think it was but I can't remember being scared! The second book I read was "Watership Down." It is a classic, very violent book. Again, nothing. In the most graphic part of the book, the rabbits are tearing one another apart. It was very, very descriptive but I was just going through the pages. I wanted to feel it. *Gosh, that is so gory, I should be gagging here.* I love reading and the feeling of seeing everything in my head, even wondering about the story while I am reading it. But how did I feel? I felt cold, nothing, not caring, turning the pages, watching the clock, trying to get through the day.

I also remember not caring about food. Everything tasted salty and metallic, like a dirty rubber washer I remember chewing as a child. Did I ever get in trouble for that one! My salivary glands were drying up. The only thing that tasted like it should were Cheetos and macaroni and cheese with broccoli. I still love that combination and Cheetos. I really can't figure out why those two things never lost their flavor. I remember stirring food around my plate, not wanting to eat because it tasted bad and it hurt to swallow (side effect), but I knew that I had to eat something. The good news was I lost a bit of weight, another happy side effect I didn't know about.

Going to the bathroom was also a challenge. It was more that I wouldn't go, rather than I couldn't go. I would sit on my bed thinking, *Man, I sure do need to go to the bathroom. I better get up and go. Wow, I have to go really badly!* However, I would just lie there and not get up. Why? I don't know. I just didn't feel like moving. So I would wait there until the last possible second, almost holding myself so I wouldn't pee all over the room. When I went, did I run? No. Did I hurry to get there? No, I would just saunter on over to pee and saunter back as if there had been no sense of urgency. Each time I thought, *oh I have to pee. Didn't I just do that a few hours ago? I really have to go . . . I better get up.* It was the same process, over and over all week long. Now that is apathy!

The only thing I really did care about was my few minutes of visit time with the nurses. These were angels on earth. Everyone there needed tending to, pills given to them, their catheter bag changed, and made as comfortable as possible. How could they do this daily? The nurses were so kind and loving. Such strong women. This was before male nurses were common. I do remember thanking my nurses for their selfless efforts and for working so hard to help me and all their patients feel better. They made me feel better spiritually as well as medically. They all had to wear the little meter that read how much radiation exposure they had for the day. Even with a low reading, they still wouldn't come into the room. However, being low for the day, they would sometimes lean on the doorframe and chat with me. I loved that. One can only take so many reruns of "Petticoat

Junction." Even the orderly who brought my food in had to wear the meter. They all said it could make them sterile. *Hmm, what was it doing to me? Could I have children?*

~Radiation Side Effects~

My muscles ached as if I was coming down with the flu. I lost my appetite and just didn't care about much. I was just so tired and felt weak, effects from the radiation. I had these terrific migraine-type headaches too. I would get sublingual meds for that. The worst part about the pills is that I had to catch my "headache" just at its peak. If I took the pill too soon, I would throw-up; if I waited too long, it didn't work and would leave me feeling worse than when I started. I would have migraines for a few years on and off. Mostly I would just endure the headache because it seemed I was always guessing wrong with those pills.

Then my mom came up with a remedy that we would later call a "potato headache." We used this term for quick execution purposes. You know, many of those remedies from old wives' tales do work. It did for me. You take a raw potato and slice it into circles about an eighth of an inch thick. Wet a washcloth with vinegar, wring out any excess, wrap the potatoes in the cloth (usually three slices), and then place it on your forehead. I would go and lie down in my bedroom. In less the thirty minutes, the headache was gone. No kidding! I don't know why it worked, just that it did. As soon as I saw the aura, I would claim a "potato headache" and either me or my mom would get it going. They finally did go away. I still tell people about the potato cure. I know it sounds funny, but it's natural and it worked wonders for me and for the others who tried it.

My list of side effects were right out of the text books, and it seems that I was adding to the list daily. Many of the things I was feeling, I didn't know were side effects. When I was getting large dosages, I got nausea and vomiting. Not a lot of throwing up, just enough to keep me busy. There was one thing I really did care about, I didn't want to make a mess everywhere for someone to clean up. Other symptoms included some chest pain and increased heart rate.

My heart would race so badly everyone had trouble counting it. I think sometimes that I could see my heart pounding in my chest. Racing heartbeat would flare up for almost two years and still occurs to this day. Not all the time and not by doing anything special, just out of the blue. Bam! My heart would start to palpitate. It didn't feel really good either. It was hard to breathe so I would cough a little bit, trying to catch my breath and wait. After a short while, my heartbeat would slow down and stabilize. The doctors said this was normal. I just accepted it as something that will happen from time to time. At first I would panic, thinking I was having a heart attack or that my heart was going to explode. I was young and didn't know any better. The doctors did tell me that I would be okay, just stay calm and they would pass. I later learned that this was sound advice.

Did I mention the sweats, very much like hot flashes? I could feel the heat spreading from my chest up to my chin. Since my neck had lost most of its feeling, that was very strange. I could feel the heat below my collarbone, then no heat, and then heat again around my chin. It was as if a paper was blocking the area I couldn't feel. Parts of my face are still numb and when the wind hits it, I still get the same feeling. Weird! My skin itched too so they got me some special cream. They said the radiation made my skin dry out, another reaction. I didn't get hives but I did get a red rash on my skin that itched. My palms also turned red, peeled, and flaked. They said that was from the anesthesia.

As I mentioned earlier, my salivary glands were affected too. I got the initial dry mouth while getting the radiation. The rest of the side effects took longer to manifest. I told the doctors my mouth would dry out and water didn't even help, like water sliding off a duck's back, sliding right down my throat not being absorbed or anything. At that time, the doctors would just blow me off. With so many people saying the same thing now, they say that certain medications may affect the saliva glands, giving the patient dry mouth. Huh, go figure! There are even products for that now. They work pretty well. I still have problems with my saliva but it's okay. Years later, my teeth began to fall out because of the radiation. Thank God for implants!

My neck hurt too. I had a sore throat most of the time. When I coughed, my stomach ached or got cramps, like I had done sit-ups or I was getting my period. I thought that was all from the surgery (some of it was) but I didn't realize that those too were signs of radiation sickness. There were just so many things I didn't know. My hair never fell out completely but it did get thin or transparent, kind of like the old ladies with blue hair. It was temporary. Good thing I had a perm! No, really, it was a good thing. It didn't look so bad.

Here are a few other things I had to endure but I either chalked it up to my surgery or just me. My stool was black. I was constipated my whole life so I just thought that was regular. Then I would have diarrhea. I would feel cold while having hot flashes. I know, this sounds just nuts. I can still be sweating with a flash and then watch my fingers turn purple from being cold. I chalk that up to the bad circulation I acquired during surgery. The worst part about this is that nobody told me that all this stuff could happen. People have even died because of the treatment.

Since my chances were so grave, the doctors did not concern themselves about that either. I don't remember if I had bruises. But for sure, I didn't have blood in my urine or stool. I didn't get all the side effects, just a few. Okay, more than a few. If my lower back or sides hurt, that was a side effect too. I thought it was from being in bed so long. But I really don't think they knew how it would affect a relatively healthy twenty-five-year-old. It was still very experimental and I was the guinea pig. Now with the invention of the Internet, there are tons of web pages with every single kind of question and side effect you could possibly think of. Since I didn't know and most of the effects could be justified, either from the surgery or being stuck in that room, I just endured. I wasn't being a martyr, I just didn't know any better.

It was time for me to leave. I was super tired and weak. Many of the major side effects were gone but they kept doing readings on me every three weeks. Mom had to keep all my stuff away from everyone until she got the okay from the doctors. I tried to do my best and not be irritable but that was a side effect too! It was hard to not be grouchy, when you are apathic. But the good news is, most of it wore off with time. I returned to my same old goofball self. When I left, I had to take the strings off my guitar because after they did the readings on me, they also checked my guitar. Sure enough, the strings' reading was too high. *Oh no, my guitar neck is going to warp.* A silly thing. I was always told to keep the tension on the neck of the guitar. *How long is too long?* I didn't know, but I needed to get home fast so I wouldn't ruin my guitar. As I was leaving, I was very happy to be worried about something. I had felt so blah, and that was an emotion! It was way better than not caring about stuff, which meant the apathy was going away.

Despite the fact that cancer became the instant driving force in my life, not being able to talk, sing, or play my guitar seemed to be my biggest fear. It was not living that concerned me, but the possible lack of not having any or all of these things in my life for however long that would be. How would I live without them? What would my life be like? I guess many twenty-five-year-olds might think that life was about sailing through the winds of change easily with a margarita in hand. Not me. I just lost the wind in my sails, and the end of the storm was nowhere in sight.

~Is That My Voice?~

Going through something like this is very much like the ebb and flow of the ocean: high tide, low tide, storms and glassy stillness. Some things trigger thoughts of past events, like when I was confronted with...

Smack! Blow one, karate chop to the throat. My folks and the doctors were standing around my bed. Dr. Schafer said, "We're not sure if she will ever speak again." *What did he just say? That I would never be able to talk? How will I communicate? How will I live? Can I still teach?* I made it through the night after my first surgery and he had just taken the tube out. This was shocking. I was devastated. I thought cancer was the problem.

Will anyone want me? Will anyone want me? Will anyone want me? Will I be a mute? Would I never say anything again? What am I going to do? Won't I make any sounds when I laugh? Oh my god, I love to laugh! Does that mean I will open my mouth and nothing will come out? My chest hurt. It was hard to breathe. *Breathe deeper, calm down.* The doctor is still talking. *Come on, Lett, focus. How long was I thinking? Are they all staring at me? Don't start crying, they will try and calm you down with drugs. I don't want more drugs! I don't like how they make me feel. Will they stick that tube down my throat again? I didn't want to go there again. With that tube in my throat, I couldn't even talk. Wait, I can't talk anyway. Well, it hurt to try!* It was awful! Grunting, squinting, and nodding are lousy ways to communicate. *I will just clear my throat. Testing, one…two…three.* Nothing. Squeak! *Wait, did I hear something? Was that my voice?* They stopped talking and looked at me. *Oh, great! They think I am getting upset because I am trying to say something and nothing is coming out. Calm down! Trust that it's going to be okay. They made a mistake. I'm twenty-five. Things like this don't happen to twenty-five-year-olds. I am a teacher. How will I do my calling? Who will want me?* I am so tired. I think I need to rest. *Oh god, I just I missed everything he said. What are they saying now? I need another surgery?* I'm so tired. *They didn't get it all? I still have cancer? They have to go back in? How much more? Can they fix my voice then?* Tired. *Who will want me? Can I laugh? Can I teach?*

Sleep rescued me. *Wow, how long was I asleep this time? The doctors were gone so a while, I guess.* My solution to this problem was to become a teacher for mute children. I didn't know how that would work but I was going to do it. Problem solved. I would go back to school when I got out of the hospital to learn sign language and then work in special education. *Wow, how did I come up with that? Was it even possible?* It didn't matter. In my mind, I adjusted my attitude. Was I happy that I was going back to school? No. But I was not ready to give up. I wanted to teach.

Whoosh! Blow two, the air just left my lungs! "Even if she talks, she will never sing again." This was after the second surgery. They believed they had gotten all of the cancer on the right side of my neck. They also heard a sound my vocal cords made, which meant I would be able to make some kind of sound. Blow one! Talk? Blow two! Sing? *Man, these things won't stop blowing up in my head!*

The verdict was still out. But for sure, a noise came from my vocal box. Okay, then I could whisper. Swish, the air is still seeping out. I can almost feel my singing voice fading away. *Who knew there was a singing and speaking part in me anyway? All right, I might not sing, but I might make some squeaky, whispery noises.* My solution (again, through sleep) was to become the world's best guitar player. The only problem was . . .

Blow three! "We think your arm should work fine. We did cut a lot of muscles out so you will need physical therapy. But again, we will have to wait and see." Ah, my favorite answer. This always meant they didn't have a clue. So far, I defied the odds, and I was really keeping them guessing. They stopped using the word never with me, it just didn't fit anymore. Many of the nevers were now strong, definite maybes, which is always better than a no! All right, so I have endured three major blows to my psyche. I might not speak, I might not sing, and I might not use my arm the same as before, but am I missing an elephant here? I had cancer and I still might die.

The second surgery was a success. It appeared as if they had gotten all of it. Things were looking good. I made a sound with my vocal cords, and my prognosis was shifting in the wind. I mostly just plowed through it. I would get scared...no, terrified at times. But the fear never consumed or crippled me. I was making plans for the future. I would go back to school to become a special ed teacher. I would learn sign language and, if possible, become the best guitar player in our music group. I was planning on living and beating this thing. I really didn't see myself dying. I'm twenty-five, for crying out loud!

These three blows were never fatal although they would become life-changing. People's lives change drastically all the time and still they live wonderfully productive lives. I knew I could do that, too. The best part is that my faith became stronger. With the grace of God, the wind died down and I landed back on my feet.

27

The Unanticipated

My friends and family had been through the wringer throughout this journey with me. Their emotions were raw, which created some very interesting times. Overreacting can really be tough sometimes, especially when you are the person they are reacting about. I can still recall two vivid memories that stick out as if they happened yesterday.

~The Plunge~

We already called the doctor and he said enough time had passed that I could get in the pool if I didn't get my neck wet. Another plan was devised, only get wet up to my shoulders. Basically, I could wade in the water. *Hey, that sounds like a song!* Lorraine's plan worked. We were getting in the pool and I am quenching my thirsty body! I couldn't wait. Scared but excited, I tiptoed in.

"She's open, she's open! Come see, come see! It's all open!" Lorraine was yelling at the top of her lungs. It had only been twenty minutes. *What was happening?* "There!" She pointed at my neck.

Panic-stricken, I froze. My dad jumped in the water, telling me to stay put. Let's just look at the scene, I'm not two nor am I drowning. To say that everyone was overreacting is to put it mildly. The way she was yelling, it sounded as if I had a gaping hole in my neck or my head was going to fall off. Dad gently grabbed me and led me to the side of the pool. I'm speechless. My brain, on the other hand, is going berserk. *Why did I say I wanted to go swimming? Well, it is ninety-eight degrees, that's a good reason. I'm always causing so much trouble. How open is open? Am I going back to the hospital?*

For some reason, I guess they thought that I was some sort of invalid (someone who couldn't take care of herself) or I had forgotten how swim. I realize why now but it never hit me then. I had been at death's door. I was so fragile, they were on edge. Swimming was a regular thing, maybe one of our first regular things. They feared I did some horrible damage to myself and we would have to start all over again. Granted, these were unfounded thoughts and fear-driven, but these kinds of things will cause illogical thinking. A little shaken up, I slowly got out of the water while they called the doctor. I decided to have a look. Sure enough, there was this white, wriggly looking thing on my neck where the stitches had been. It did look like there was an opening there, a tiny little hole about the size of a small nailhead. *Oh my god, my neck insides are squishing out! What did I just do?* It appeared all white and spongy, kind of gross, really. Mom sent me off to get dressed in case I needed to get to the doctor. We were in go mode, a now well-practiced and rehearsed method. We sat sweating (it still was ninety-eight degrees) in the living room. Nobody was talking. The phone rang, Mom jumped up. This was before cordless phones were invented.

She answered in the kitchen but we could hear her. "Yes, doctor, she's fine. No, she's in no pain. No, it doesn't appear to be oozing, a little open hole, spongy with a tiny white thing sticking out." An eternal pause. *Was I going back to the hospital?* He knew I had been in the pool because he gave me permission. The doctor surmised that a bit of stitch they had missed must've gotten wet. He told my mom not to worry about it and he'd see me that week. Keep it dry, keep me calm, and no more swimming until after he saw me! Mom chuckled with relief, "Okay, doctor, she won't!" *I won't what?* "Thank you so much. Okay, see you later this week." Crisis averted. Ta-da!

I recovered. Being in the pool will always be something I remember, sort of a milestone and major step in my recovery, terrifying but only briefly. It felt so good and refreshing, liberating and normal. I can remember everyone watching me with anticipation as I stepped into the pool. The best part was just being in the water—

splashing, chatting, and laughing just like any regular day in the pool! Once I knew that I had conquered the pool, I knew that I could conquer anything. It was scary. My heart was racing and everyone went into panic mode, but the significance of that event was a major lesson for us all.

~The Masses of the Mass~

My second vivid memory was not going to the circus, but more like creating my own. When you go to a circus, it's very exciting—the lights, the sounds, the smell, the animals, and the people. For me, going to church for the first time in several months was very much like a three-ring circus and I was the main event. I can remember getting there already feeling weak and thinking going there was a mistake. As soon as I got out of the car, people started saying, "Letty's here! Letty's here!"

My parents had been founding members of St. Pius. In the tenth grade, I started singing there. My mom used to pick me up for music practice until I started driving myself. I had been singing at mass for ten years every Sunday without fail, except when I went to Barranquilla for a year and when I was in the hospital. I was pretty well known. The congregation and I had created a bond together. When I showed up that day, I was bombarded. People were hugging me, though they didn't know they were unintentionally hurting me. Some were crying, laughing, and staring. They looked at me with true joy and relief. I had beaten the odds. Their prayers had been heard. Here is a living, breathing miracle!

Oh my god, what is happening? This is too much! Can we please go home now? I wanted to run away and hide. It was so overwhelming. I wasn't singing, I wasn't even standing with my group. I was just sitting in a pew at the front. People came by my pew grabbing my hand, touching me, and looking at me in disbelief. It was like a reception line. *Whew! This is way harder than I thought it would be.* I sighed, letting a puff of air escape me. I catch Joe's eyes, I look at him pleadingly, *Okay, somebody start mass, please!* So many tears. Finally, everything started to settle down, and I thought I could relax. The opening song began with my beloved group singing: Joe on upright bass; Tom, Mike, and Lorraine on guitar; Pat on the percussion; and Kathy, Donna, Pops, and Laura on vocals. It was a beautiful sight, eyes shining and voices singing. I started to tear up because it had been so overwhelming. *Ugh!* The lump in my throat ached from not crying. *I can't cry, they are all watching. It will just make them cry more.* I took a deep breath and then another one. *Breathe, Lett, you can do this.* We all sat down. *Ah, that feels great. Wow, I didn't realize my knees were shaking! It's okay, just relax.*

Father Kulleck gave the opening prayer. He proudly looked at me, smiled, and then said in his booming voice, "We would all like to welcome back our Letty." More tears, clapping, cheering, and standing! *They are standing? What did I do? I didn't do anything.* I wanted to crawl under the pew. It felt extremely excessive. I was doing everything I could to keep myself from bursting out crying. My mother grabbed my hand and told me to breathe. Joe was just beaming. It was as if I had won the Nobel Peace Prize. *This is too much! When would mass start and get the attention off me? Please start the mass and just leave me alone! Stop looking at me, I look awful!* The stitches had been out for a while but the scar was bright-red, jagged, and thick as my middle finger. You could even see the little holes where the stitches had been. I felt like my head was jutting out and was off center for sure. I was off center. *Please take me home, this was a mistake! It's too much. I just wanted to go to church. Thank you, God, for letting me survive, have Eucharist, be with everyone, be able to thank them for their prayers, and hear my group sing, but that's all. That's all. Not this. Please stop!* It was agony.

Finally, it did stop and all attention was diverted back to the mass. The good news is that the mass is only an hour and fifteen minutes long. I made it. I was still weak, and my family was still tired from everything. None of my family members expected that kind of welcome. Even they got dizzy from all the attention and love. There must have been two hundred people who congratulated me, hugged me, touched me, or cried over me. The mass ended. *Thank you, God!* After more hugs and tears, signing a few autographs (just kidding), and collapsing into the car, we remarked how incredible that had been. I think I fell asleep midsentence. I slept the rest of the day and the next day too.

The following week, we snuck into the church late and sat in the little room where the altar boys change. My dad called ahead, and they had set up a few chairs for us. We came late and left early. I did that for a while until I could face that again. When I did return, I had my guitar in hand and my group members surrounding me for protection. *Thank you, God!* I knew I had to go. I felt compelled to be there for them as they had prayed so hard. I needed to say thank you for all the love and support they gave me, but we can't always control how we act. When everyone is showing you attention, it is wonderful for some, but for me, it was overwhelming, tiring, and confusing. We give and take energy from each other all day so when it comes in such a large quantity it is a lot to take in and although extremely wonderful, it was overpowering.

The congregation's over-the-top expression of love caused such confusion for me. I felt like I had done nothing to deserve it. But for people of faith, I was proof of their prayers, of miracles, and of God's love for us. By surviving, I had become a symbol of hope. That is what I did with the grace of God. I didn't get it then but I understand it now.

28

Five Years down the Road

HOT SPOTS? I AM RIDDLED with them. There are little dots all in my gut. Was it cancer again? They all seem to think so. I thought so. *Wow, that was fast! Five years down the line and here I am, wearing this drafty gown again as I'm watching the same tiles roll by.* The orderly wheels me closer to the surgery room. *Has it really been five years?*

I'm talking, singing, teaching, and traveling. Hey, I just got back from a whole summer in Tlaxcala, Mexico, from a course in Bilingual Education. That was so much fun, even if I was flooding like a river. I can't really remember when my period became so heavy or when the fist-sized clots began. It just crept up on me. They had been monitoring me, watching for any signs of cancer with scans, scopes, and blood every six months. After the first year, when they said I was cancer-free, they were really saying that the cancer was gone but... "Let's wait and see," said the doctors. "If you make it to five years, it will definitely improve your chances of survival." *I wonder why they don't paint stuff on the ceiling tiles. There are so many patients rolling by every day, every hour, and every minute. Hmm, just how many tiles are up there?*

I remember going to see Dr. Wilder, my OB-GYN. She was very concerned. Aside from the tremendous amount of bleeding, I had a large mass about the size of an orange near my lower intestine. She found it during an exam and was alarmed. She set the date for surgery soon after. I was also anemic and weak. My periods were lasting fifteen to seventeen days a month with heavy bleeding and clotting. *So here I am again. Did I get my e-ticket for this ride? Am I even ready for this thing?* Surgery has got to be better than gripping a chair, waiting for the clot to pass, and then rushing to the bathroom as a stream of blood flowed from me. I was depleted each time that happened. How much longer could my body hold out? There was always so much blood. I wore a double pad most of time and it still soaked through when the gushing would start. Sometimes in the classroom, I would have to call the office for help. They all knew.

Willow School was small then, only twenty teachers. We knew each other well. We called ourselves the Willow family. We were close friends, seeing each other and doing social things after hours. We really felt like family. I went to live with Patricia in Coronado, California. What a great time we had, we just hit it off. We both worked at Willow. She was single; I was single. We had money, time, and a love for travelling. Those years just flew by after my cancer surgeries. I was singing at St. Pius, still working at Willow, and having a wonderful life. Other than my prolonged menstrual cycles, my health had been good.

The word had gotten out again that I needed surgery. It looked like I had cancer again. Every test indicated colon cancer. It even looked like I was going to get a colostomy, which is a piece of your gut diverted to an opening in your abdominal wall, then you pooped through that into a bag. *I'm thirty and I was being prepped to wear a poop bag. Good-bye marriage!* The week before surgery, my diet consisted of Jell-O, chicken broth, castor oil, and citric nitrate. They told me they wanted the intestines as clean as a whistle, which meant no solid foods for a week. They were going to cut the cancerous part of my intestine out and then sew me back together.

I remember trying to choke back the green Jell-O. I was in my Coronado apartment, choking back tears. I think it was a Wednesday and I already had three days of this junk. I'm on the sofa, looking at the jiggly stuff. *What am I doing? Why am I doing this? Do I really have cancer again? Am I going to die this time? Can I eat one more spoonful of this junk? I'm gonna gag.* I did gag as I finished the gelatinous globs of artificial, lime flavored swill. *Oh God!* I cover my mouth with my hand. *I almost lost it all on that one!* Gag! Gag! Gag!

I persevered through the rest of the week. Ugh! I spent most of the time in the bathroom because "clean as a whistle" means no poop inside me at all! Nothing. Nada. Not a glob! Needless to say, I was sore everywhere you can think of and maybe some places you can't think of. I remember talking to my priest. Fr. Kulleck told me there is life after a colostomy. People lead relatively normal lives after that. Regardless, I was pretty sad. Not only did they say I had cancer again, but now I would never go to the bathroom like a regular person—that is, if the cancer didn't kill me this time. I was in that five-year mark Dr. Schafer talked about, now I had all those hot spots. During the MRI, I was given a contrast dye. The dye is absorbed by anything that's not supposed to be there. I definitely had spots clustered in my colon. Cancer. This time, I asked if I could see the MRI. Did I know what I was looking for? Did I know what cancer looked like on that thing? No. As I am staring at the picture, I knew. *I see dots, big ones the size of a tack. There are less than a dozen; still, they aren't supposed to be there. Now what? I have cancer again.* This is bad, really bad. Again, little dots of sweat form on my brow.

The day of the surgery was scary. I had already gone to several classes about "how to clean, and not throw-up, each time you have to change the bag and how to live with a bag clamped to your side." I was ready. Or was I? Was anyone really? This was going to change my life forever. By the way, how long was forever? Just how bad was my cancer?

Ceiling tiles roll by…one, two—ah, the calming drug was taking effect. Hmm was I going to float again? Was that even real? Dr. Wilder called in three or four extra doctors to do the surgery. With my history and everything the tests indicated, she wanted to be sure they were ready for anything. There was an oncologist, a doctor for the colostomy, another doctor for I'm-not-sure-what, and then her. She said I had a very bad case of endometriosis, which caused the heavy bleeding. She said I also had a number of tumors and cysts. They would try not to do a complete hysterectomy because I was so young and not married. They would try to save what they could so I could maybe have children. *Children? What about marriage? Who will want me?*

I did my part. I had eaten so much Jell-O I was Jell-O-sized or maybe I was a gel-a-ton. Again, I came to terms with the ordeal.

Throughout those five years, I started talking to people about their cancer. I enjoyed talking with them. The more I talked, the better everything got. My faith was stronger than ever, and I truly believed I was kept alive for a reason. *Was this it? Was it to teach? Was it to minister? To sing? No to that one.* Although I developed a great ability to sing harmony, my day job of teaching would remain a source of my steady income and singing would forever be my deepest form of prayer. Maybe that's why I wasn't too freaked out about the surgery. Maybe this was the end. Then again, maybe not. Fr. Kulleck said people live regular lives. Okay, so I didn't take any vows of chastity or anything, but I was living the life and I was ministering to people. So maybe I was like a modern-day nun without a habit! I could do that. I was sure that no one would want a woman with a huge scar on her neck, a giant scar running down from her navel to her private parts, and a big old bag strapped to her side! Okay, so a nun's life it is; only, I would have more freedom than a nun has and more money!

Let's get this over with! Just how long is this hallway anyway? As it turned out, the doctors stormed out of the operating room. They were livid with Dr. Wilder. She was kind of giggling when she told me. They literally pulled all my guts out onto a table and were looking desperately to find the cancer! They found tons of endometriosis, grape-like clusters of tumors and cysts. They took out one ovary and tube that had been destroyed, but there was no evidence of cancer! Nothing. Nada. Not a speck. They demanded to know why their time was being wasted. They were important doctors. She was laughing as she told me how pompous they were. She understood. She did her homework though. Not every test could have been wrong. I had cancer. Where did it go? It just wasn't there! Should she have told me about the reaction of those other doctors? Probably not, but we developed a bond. We talked about faith. She understood that some things were not in our control. She would always say, "We are doctors, not God!" Check mark. I had just received another miracle!

Good old St. Pius did it again. They rallied the troops, began the rosaries at night, and prayed up a storm. *Man, that prayer wheel was strong! A direct line.* I was fine. No poop bag, no cancer, and only one ovary was gone! I hit the jackpot again. *Wow, incredible!* God's plan for me continued. I was to tell my story of hope to as many people as would listen. I would share…no, scream about His work to anyone who would listen. That's what it has been for so many years, so many people, so many prayers, and so many tears. Some have died; some have lived. I never have the answers. Whatever I say comes from the Holy Spirit, especially if it's good stuff. It's never for me to question, only to be there for them. What a blessing!

29

Conversion

I KNOW JUST WHEN THE conversion happened. I was sitting at a work-shop, listening to our favorite music group, the Dameans. My music group, the Sounds of the Son had cut an album as a fund-raiser to bring the famous singing priests out to sunny San Diego. They were going to give a workshop on music and then give us a concert that evening.

It's hard to believe that I had started in music ministry in 1968 and didn't even know it. I got to get out of class to develop my skills. Groovy! Now it was 1980, and the Contemporary Christian Music scene was on the move, drums and all. I was very much a part of that scene. It was a good time. I was singing, still being cool, and just starting to touch the inner beauty of the music. Our new, soon-to-be rock star friends were coming. It would be so exciting to hang around and get to know them. These guys were the real deal. *Hey, if they were the real deal, then did that mean we were rock stars too?*

The day finally arrived, there were about eighty people from all around the diocese. Of course, St. Pius had the most people there. I mean, we had six music groups, from the traditional old folk's choir-organ style to us, the contemporary guitars-and-percus-sion-group. Daryl from the Dameans had been talking about music and how it was seen as a ministry. *Really, a ministry? I thought we were just being cool.* First of all, this concept of lay ministry was a new thing in the church. Things were changing because of Vatican II, and the effects were finally reaching us. Lay people (not ordained) were getting to do all kinds of things during the mass. In order to become lay ministers, worship leaders attended special classes and were commissioned to perform specific duties on behalf of the church, such as doing the first and second readings from the Bible, saying or singing the Responsorial Psalm, and distributing communion, which was the biggest deal ever. No one had ever done that except the priest. Father Ducote—or Daryl, as we later called him—kept calling it a ministry. But how was this a ministry? I just couldn't grasp the concept that I would be seen as a music minister like all those other lay leaders. We weren't church ministers, we were just singing in church.

During the workshop, Daryl had us write a letter to God. *A letter to God? What do I say? Oh my, is someone going to read this? I'm such an awful writer. What will people think?* This was so new, so innovative. We were very excited. I never heard of writing a letter to God. He then instructed us to include all the things we were thankful for and where we saw our future in this new ministry. *There it was again—ministry. What were we getting ourselves into?*

This was going to be a pretty heavy letter to God. My head was already starting to whirl. I could sense a change in the room. The mood was set for writing as they played music, which was perfect, soft, and gentle. There were no words. The lights even seemed softer, and everyone got quiet very quickly. It really put me in a very vulnerable spot. It felt like I was the only one in the church or in my pew. I immediately started to write. It was amazing just how quickly it came pouring out. I couldn't write fast enough. I knew what I wanted to tell him, what I wanted to thank him for, and how I saw myself in the future with this new ministry. I had been inspired. It was a true God moment.

> *Dear God,*
> *Where do I start? So much has happened to me. I know the first thing I want to thank you for is my life. You know, God, I never really thought I was going to die. But sometimes, maybe deep, deep inside, I might have questioned your plan for me. But here I sit with pen in hand, loving what I am*

doing. I'm teaching, playing my guitar, and, God, I am actually singing! Yeah, me! After they said I wouldn't even talk. You showed them, didn't you?

I'm sorry. I guess it's kind of ungrateful of me, but my new voice is very weird. It doesn't sound like it used to. I just don't recognize the actual voice coming out of me. It's so low, I get a little embarrassed. I know I shouldn't. It's just that sometimes I sound like a mosquito or Lou Rawles. I mean, I'm singing, for Pete's sakes! I need to give it time. I promise I will try and get used to it.

Maybe, Lord, by losing my voice, I have discovered a new one. Not just actual voice, but a new spiritual voice. Is that how this works? I also want to thank you for making my arm strong enough to play again. I'm sorry to say that I was worried about that one. It was really hard to coordinate my arm, fingers, and brain again. But I did, only because you, my friends, and family pushed me. With that gift, I promise I will practice and always be ready to play your music when needed. My guitar has always been something I have loved for years and I would have missed playing it drastically. But now, God, I cannot get enough of it. I love my guitar!

Lastly, I want to thank you for all the people who loved and supported me through this. God, I still see those cards all the time. It is overwhelming the love they gave me. I know I wasn't the best patient in the world but they still stood by me. I think for sure my mom will join the ranks of saints in heaven because of my cancer.

God, I don't know why I got cancer. I know you didn't give it to me as a punishment. I guess I am to learn something from this. Since I'm a teacher, maybe I can teach from this experience. Be patient with me, I not getting it yet. Lord, I got a gift from cancer that I never would have expected. I'm talking to people with cancer. If that's something you want me to do, I'll keep doing it. It was a bit scary at first, but it felt so good after I finished talking to them. I can see me doing this for a long time too. I know you always will give me the right words to say.

I didn't die, God. I didn't. I don't know what my future will hold. Is the cancer really gone? Will it come back? Will it be worse than the first time? Only you know this. Give me courage to face whatever comes. I know I can do it. You helped me the first time. I felt you so close to me so many times. You never left my side.

I promise with all my heart to keep on doing this ministry for as long as I can. The Dameans made it sound like it's never going away. All right, God, I'm yours—low, foreign voice; tired, heavy arm; and all. Thank you, my dear Lord.

Your servant,
Letty

Then Daryl said a magical thing. "I want you to read this letter as if God has written it to you."

What? I did not hold back. I dumped everything into it, my whole heart and soul. Tears were flowing freely. I was now aware of everything. I was back in church, the pews were full of people, my friends all saw me…they knew why I was crying. I had to stop; it still hurt too much to cry.

I began to read. Oh my god, there was so much love there! He didn't hold back either.

Dearest Letty,
So much has happened to you. The first thing I want to thank you for is trusting me with your life. You know, Letty, I knew you really never thought you were going to die. But sometimes, maybe deep,

deep inside, you might have questioned my plan for you. That's okay, I understand. But here you sit with pen in hand, loving what you're doing. You're teaching, playing your guitar, and, Letty, you are actually singing! Yeah, you. After they said you wouldn't even talk. We showed them, didn't we?

I'm sorry about your voice. You are not being ungrateful. I know your new voice is very weird to you. You're right, it doesn't sound like it used to and you don't recognize the physical voice coming out of you. It is so much lower. I understand that you get a little embarrassed. I know, it's okay. You don't really sound like a mosquito, but maybe just a bit like Lou Rawles. But, Letty, you are singing, for Pete's sake! Give it time. Thank you for your promise to try and get used to it.

Maybe, Letty, by losing your voice, you did discover a new one. Not just an actual voice, but a new spiritual voice. Yes, that's how this works. I also want to thank you for working so hard on making your arm strong enough to play. I understand that you were worried about that one. No need to apologize. It really was hard work to coordinate your arm, fingers, and brain. But you did it because of your trust in me, your friends, and family who pushed you. I know you will keep your promise with your new refound gift. I see you practicing, always ready to play my music when needed. Your guitar has always been something you loved for years, and I would have missed hearing it drastically. But now, Letty, I cannot get enough of it. I love your guitar!

Lastly, I want to thank you for allowing all the people, who loved and supported you, into your life. Letty, I still see those cards all the time too! It is so pleasing for me to see and feel the love they gave you. You know, you weren't the worst patient in the world. It made me so happy that they stood by you. Your mom will join the ranks of saints in heaven because of your cancer and so many more things.

You are right, Letty. Bodies can sometimes betray us, but I didn't give you cancer as a punishment. I would never do that. You are right again when you say you are to learn something from this. Because you are a teacher, perhaps you can teach from this experience. Be patient with me, I'm not done yet. Yes, you will get it. Letty, thank you for receiving your new gifts from cancer, not everyone would do that. That's what I love about you, you are talking and sharing with people about cancer. Oh yes, please keep doing it. I knew it was a bit scary at first, but you would feel so good after you finished talking to them. It is exciting for me to see you do this service for many years to come. The Holy Spirit will always give you the right words to say.

You didn't die, Letty. You didn't! You have so much trust because you don't know what your future will hold. Is the cancer really gone? Will it come back? Will it be worse than the first time? My child, these are all good questions. You are right, only I know. But I will give you courage to face whatever comes next. I know you can do it. I helped you the first time. You felt me so close to you so many times because of your faith. I will never leave your side.

Again, it makes me so happy that you promised with all your heart to keep on doing this ministry for as long as you can. This ministry is here to stay, it won't go away. Letty, I am yours and you are mine. I accept you with your weird; low, foreign voice; tired, heavy arm and all. Thank you, my dear Letty.

Your loving God and biggest fan,

P.S. You made it! You are my rock star.

The whole room was a sea of tears. We shared and listened to each other. We hugged, laughed, and cried. It was a beautiful morning, one that I will never forget. These guys were incredible. How did they know how to do all this newfangled, modern stuff? *Wow, I feel like I left a puddle of blood in the pew from the depths of my thoughts! Good thing no person or animal was harmed in the writing of this letter and no blood was shed that day from anyone in the church.* I checked just to make sure.

A bond had been set that day. We were all music ministers now. We had a newfound purpose, we would still be cool. But more than that, we were proclaiming the Word of God in music. We were there to help the congregation sing His praises through song. I never thought of our music as a ministry, yet now I was forever changed. I had said so much to God and He to me! I just experienced a spiritual conversion, and I didn't even realize how it would affect the rest of my life. I was on my way. I was a music minister. Reflecting on the many years, tunes, tears, laughter, pain, sorrow, and cool fun, this ministry has made me feel like taffy at times. In order to be sweet, soft, and wonderful, it has to be stretched. Sometimes it is stretched to the breaking point, only to be mended again and then stretched even further. I wouldn't give up one second of being pushed and pulled after all these years. It has helped me make the music even sweeter, richer, and more filling. I made it! I am a rock star! *Wait, isn't that what God said so many years back?*

30

Faith and Music

Watch your thoughts, they become your words.
Watch your words, they become your actions.
Watch your actions, they become your habits.
Watch your habits, they become your character.
Watch your character, it becomes your destiny

—Anonymous

WE ALL SAW THE MOVIE where the hero had just gotten out of the mouth of the cave and a small stone had been kicked down off the side of the cliff on to nothing. It stopped and appeared to be floating on air. He wondered about getting to the other side. What was he supposed to do, walk on air? There seemed no way to get across. The chasm was too deep to see the bottom and too wide to throw a rock across. Trust. Was he supposed to just take a step off the side? Take that leap of faith? Okay, the book said to take the unseen path, to walk the straight and narrow.

Really? Is that it? Just walk off the cliff? He grabs his heart, doubt grabs him. He takes a deep breath, raises his foot and steps down, into what appears to be air. As he walks the path is revealed, it had been there all along. Incredible! There is a pathway to the other side. It's about a foot wide and very straight. He will literally have to walk the straight and narrow. He takes a deep breath and walks. It is terrifying. He had filled his pockets with everything he could find to fling in his pathway. He had to be wise and conservative with the

190

debris to make sure he had enough to throw so he could see to get across. One false step and he would plummet to his death. Now that is faith!

Of course, our character is Indiana Jones from the 1989 film, 'Indiana Jones and the Last Crusade'. This blockbuster had so many signs of faith, it's a wonder that it didn't get categorized as a religious thriller! This particular scene stuck with me long after I saw it, even to this day. It was so powerful that it has stirred my soul with those profound images of his leap of faith.

My foundations had been moved. I guess cancer can do that to you. I'm a Cradle Catholic, and I was fine with just going about my Catholic duties. I received the sacraments, went to church, and even did a little extra like singing at mass. But I was just going through the motions.

"Faith is taking the first step even when you don't see the staircase" (Martin Luther King Jr.). That seems like Indy. He was literally stepping out in faith. "Faith consists in believing when it is beyond the power of reason to believe" (Voltaire). Luke 17:6 (The New American Bible) says, "If you have faith as small as a mustard seed, you could say to the sycamore, 'Be uprooted and transplanted in the sea,' and it will obey you." In other words, if you had the same amount of faith as the teeny, tiny mustard seed it would be a sufficient amount to accomplish anything. That is a pretty awesome image of what we could do with a tiniest amount of true of faith.

We should put our trust in God and believe that there is an individual plan for each of us. Sometimes it doesn't turn out as we wish. Here's where the lesson lies. How do we react? What do we do with the outcome? It also means we have to have trust, hope, and belief in goodness. We believe in the reality that things will turn out well at the end of an event. There never is a guarantee for anything, but it's that faith that keeps us moving. In a retreat I attended author Anne Trufant said, "Ask God to help you have the desire to have the desire." Sometimes all we can do to move forward is just want to move forward. That's okay, it's a start in the faith direction!

The question that always comes up is why can the doctors heal some and not all? I survived, because it wasn't my time, even though all the physical variables lined up. All those prayers were answered because God was developing my character so that I would go out to tell people about this miraculous story of hope.

Watch your character, it becomes your destiny.

—Anonymous

Part 3

Not the End

31

It's Not Really the End

Do I REALLY HAVE THE light of Christ in me? I sure hope so. Cancer has given me the opportunity to let more people see, feel, and experience the light of Christ in order to give hope. When did that all change for me? When did I stop waiting for that other shoe to fall? When did my transformation take place and I let go and let God take over? *Okay, Lett, you can do this. But what if I say the wrong thing? You don't know anything about anything!*

I heard that an acquaintance from church and theater who sang in the eight o'clock choir had breast cancer. I made up my mind to visit with her. It had almost been a year since my last surgery and I was strong, singing at church and teaching at Willow School. She was an older woman, well past fifty.

I rang the bell. *Why is my heart pounding and my stomach fluttering?* I remember a very clear picture of the older homes in Chula Vista. There was no sidewalk in front of her house. It had an antique look to it, a Victorian type of house with gray and purple paint. It even had an attic. It had no storage place above the garage but a real attic with a cool ladder that you pulled down. Very few homes in San Diego had real attics. It was just like everything you read about in a storybook. We walked up the old creaking stairs in silence. *Where is she taking me?*

As if hearing my thoughts, she said, "Oh, I just want to show you something." She opened the door and a musty smell enveloped me. There before me appeared in a giant room filled with every

195

type of costume and prop you could ever want organized by time periods.

I put my hand to my heart and said, "Oh my god!" I couldn't believe what I was looking at. Mrs. T was known for doing local theater every summer at St. Pius. She was the keeper of the costumes and props. *I wonder if it's a sin to covet all these costumes. I just have to touch this one.* It was a beautiful shimmering, fully-beaded, aquamarine 1920s flapper dress complete with a fringe. I just had to see it move. It felt rich and old at the same time. This was how she was letting me into her life. There we sat for hours in old cane chairs among old clothes long forgotten, talking about cancer. I recall her telling me she didn't know where all this would go and wondering if she would die from cancer. She started telling me her fears and doubts. I knew how she was feeling, I had been there. In fact, I was still there. She was one of those who prayed for my recovery. *I remember your cards, Mrs. T.* I was there because of God's grace!

I lost track of time. I remember deeply listening to her, mostly answering questions as they came. It wasn't time for my story. This was her time. I was relaxed and felt really calm and peaceful. My mom knew where I was so I wasn't concerned that she would worry. I went in the morning and it was about mid-afternoon when I left. *I feel like I'm floating on air. Oh my god, is this what you want me to do to help people with cancer?* I knew it was the right thing to do. Mrs. T gave me such a warm, reassuring hug, thanking me and asking me to come back again. Later on, she would tell me how hopeful she felt. I have always said, "If I said something really powerful to you, it wasn't me, it was the Holy Spirit." I was glowing and couldn't get home fast enough to tell my mom.

It had been months since I had yelled—well, I really didn't yell because if I did try, my voice would catch and then I would start to cough—but I did come in louder than usual. "I'm home!" It had also been months since my mom saw the true Letty.

When I came crashing through the door, needless to say, my mom was shocked and startled. She was not expecting the old Letty. She was expecting the quieter version of myself. She said it was music to her ears; the crashing was fantastic! Something wonderful had just happened to her Letty. Mom was welling up with joy because Loud Letty was back. It really was quite an unspoken moment. She was in the kitchen when she dried her hands, grabbed mine, and pulled me to the living room sofa. She said, "Tell me what happened, Letty. Are you okay?"

I noticed the anticipation shining in her eyes. I then began to reveal my morning to her. I could hardly talk, I was so excited. Mom never really spoke of that moment until years later. If she was going to say something to me about feeling good to see the old Letty back, I just didn't let her. Like a whirlwind, I just plowed through the door. I was on fire! "I know why God had saved me! I now have my purpose. I can talk to people with cancer!"

When I started telling my mom about my experience, she says I was radiant, that she had never seen me so beautiful. She did see the light of Christ in me and I believed her. I felt it then and still do, nearly every time I talk to a person with cancer.

Before I knew it, I was talking to a second and then a third person. Both of those women had recurring cancer several times. They fought the good fight, but in the end, their jobs were complete and God sent for them. I learned so much of life and death from these courageous women. I was weak at times and would doubt my new mission. *Why did I live and they died?* Thankfully, the message has always been very clear as years went by—share, share, and share your story. It provides strength, courage, belief, and hope. I have talked to people all around the world, from coast to coast. They were mostly women and mostly Christian, but I got all kinds too. Whoever asks, I will listen and I will talk. My mom always said, "You don't have to tell them every intimate detail." But I would say, "Yes, I do. If they ask, I will not hold back. If they have cancer, there are so many questions that the doctors won't have time to address. It is the least I can do. I have a license to say things others can't.

My dear Lord, you did this. You have given me the right words every time. You have given me the gifts of understanding, compassion, and empathy. Thank you so much.

Epilogue

Down the Road

ALMOST FORTY YEARS LATER, I have lived a rich, full life. My faith remained steadfast; my music true. I taught for thirty-three fantastic years. I was an ambassador of education to Africa, sponsored by the Rotary Club. I was Teacher of the Year for San Diego County. I even made it to the top twenty-five teachers in the state of California. I've been on television several times and had my kindergarten students, the ABC Rockers, perform in front of thousands of people, even for a senator's inauguration. I cut six albums. I was blessed to purchase my own condominium and later a house with Gary. I have traveled the world with my family and friends, Jen, Janet, and Olivia. I love to sing and play my guitar at retreats. I can ski, snorkel, hike, and take long walks. I'd say that's a fantastic life of nearly forty extra years. But the best part was that I found my partner, my love, and best friend in my Gary, a man who has enhanced my life beyond my expectations.

It seems God always creates a path for me to meet with people with cancer, no matter how busy I get. I have talked to hundreds, perhaps even thousands of people, sometimes one-on-one and other times in groups. Wherever I am called, I will go.

In the spring of 2015, I was asked to do a talk at a Cursillo. This is a Catholic movement meant to enrich and deepen our lives with Christ. The retreat lasts from Thursday to late Sunday and I was to speak on Sunday. My talk was based on my cancer journey and the numerous miracles that transpired because of it. I was nearly finished and was getting to the part about the I-131 protocol. When I got to that part, I said, "So anyone who has any type of a lymphatic papillary carcinoma will now receive some form of the I-131."

There off to my left, a woman raises her hand and softly speaks. "Thank you." There was stirring at her table, electricity was in the air.

At first, I wasn't sure what she had said. It took a full two or three seconds to sink in. *Wait what did she say? Why was she thanking me? What did I do?* Wait for it…*Oh my god! She had the I-131! She is thanking me because I did the experiment! Is she crying? Am I crying? Of course we are crying!*

Suddenly, it was just the two of us in a room of 129 people. Everyone vanished. Our eyes locked. I wanted to memorize her face so that when we broke into small groups, I would be able to find here. Derailed! The rest of my talk was lost. I said out loud, "Wait, what just happened? This isn't part of my talk. Did you guys just hear that? She just thanked me because of the I-131! Did you hear that? This is not part of my talk." I was definitely off script now.

Whispers and buzzing burst in the room. Murmurs, talks, gasps, tears, and laughter seem to float from table to table. Then all at once, the crowd started clapping. We just stood there in awe. *Did someone give the cue to clap? How did they all know when to start? What just happened? What am I supposed to do now? Do I finish? Do I run up to her and hug her? Am I finished with my talk?* I tried to say something but it was gone flat out. No noise. Nothing. Nada! I cleared my throat, swallowed hard, and then said, "Oh my god! This is not part of my talk. Just so you know, she's not a plant. I didn't know she was going to do that."

This was very true. Rarely, if ever, is the speaker interrupted. Her response to my talk was very spontaneous and heartfelt. She had to let me know right then and there that she was sitting there because of me. Incredible! I somehow got back on track and quickly finished my talk. As soon as it was over, people stood up and clapped. There were laughter and tears. She came up to me. We hugged and cried for the longest time. It was clearly a moment none of us will ever forget. Later, we spoke at great length. She shared many of her thoughts and fears and now grace. Somehow my talk had freed her from her fears of the cancer. Even after all of these years, my cancer still remains a blessing. I don't question it any longer. This was the biggest God moment I had ever experienced. God knew just what he was doing, and He orchestrated this from the start. It was very unusual that I should be asked to do this very same talk twice in a row. There are many wonderful talks and speakers yet the rectora, or leader for the retreat, felt compelled to ask me to do it again. I almost declined. I told her, "You want me to do it again? I just did it in October. Are you sure? I can talk on something else if you like."

Her response was to tell me to pray on it. I did. As if smacked on the head, I remembered that I would never say no to this talk no matter how many times I have given it. Every time I tell this story, there is a different emphasis on some part. I never know why I will include certain parts of my story or omit certain parts. Then after it is revealed to me by someone who heard the talk, I understand. It always makes sense. Sometimes I don't get to find out why particular parts are emphasized. Rarely do I have notes, I just tell the story. I don't question anymore. I trust that God always makes sense. Why did I hesitate this time? I really don't know. It took less than day to realize that I needed to tell the story again even if some of the women already heard it. There might be one person who needed to hear it at that time.

There I stood with that one person. The realization came crashing down on me. He did it again! After so many years of this ministry, it is still amazing how God is using me. What a blessing! What a life! What a gift! Where will this take me? Only God knows. My job is to stay open, to be His vessel, and share my story of faith, music, and cancer.

About the Author

ALMOST FORTY YEARS AFTER SHE survived cancer when all the odds were against her, Letty Rocha-Peck continues to make every moment of her life count by praising God and thanking Him for the gift of time.

She began her teaching career in Barranquilla, Colombia, South America. She spent the remaining thirty-two years in the San Ysidro School District, a stone's throw from the US-Mexican border in San Diego, California. She represented the district as Teacher of the Year as well as San Diego County on the state level. Along with a select group of teachers, she traveled to Africa, representing and exemplifying public education in Southern California. She earned a master's degree in child-centered psychology while remaining a weekly music minister at St. Pius X in Chula Vista.

She was instrumental in bringing the performing arts to every child at Willow School by hosting weekly sing-alongs, overseeing a quarterly reading rally, as well as organizing and planning yearly musical productions that incorporated both science and social studies curriculum standards. Over the years, Letty has recorded both childrens and Christian music. She continues to sing and play for regular retreats throughout the year. Frequently, she is asked to speak about her cancer experience at retreats and to cancer patients. Letty never hesitates to volunteer because she is convinced that God fills the venue with just the right people who need to hear about the miracle of her healing and the faith that gave her the strength to endure.

Letty lives with her husband Gary in the community of Bonita, California. She remains active in music ministry at Mater Dei Catholic Parish and enjoys traveling as often as possible. She will continue to share God's grace and love everywhere she goes.

CPSIA information can be obtained
at www.ICGtesting.com
Printed in the USA
FSHW021533060419
56969FS